THE ART OF DRYING PLANTS AND FLOWERS

The
Art of Drying
Plants and Flowers

Mabel Squires

BONANZA BOOKS · NEW YORK

*This edition published by Gramercy Publishing Company,
a division of Crown Publishers, Inc.,
by arrangement with William Morrow and Company, Inc.*
L   M   N

© MCMLVIII by Mabel Squires

Printed in the United States of America.

Library of Congress Catalog Card No. 58-8160

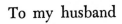

To my husband

Acknowledgments

I wish to express my appreciation and gratitude to the following people who helped in putting this book together: to Mr. Richard Farnum, Executive Secretary, The Horticultural Society of New York, who gave me the idea that I could do a book on my favorite hobby; to Mrs. Enid Grote, Librarian, The Horticultural Society of New York, who helped and encouraged me during the several years I spent writing it; and to my husband whose untiring assistance led to its completion.

Contents

THE ART OF DRYING PLANTS AND FLOWERS

Introduction

The drying of plants is a fascinating hobby. Anyone can participate in this decorative art since it does not take expert skill nor require elaborate equipment. A lack of experience need not deter you and if you do ruin a few pieces the first time it is no serious matter, for you will soon get into the swing of it. Once the fundamentals are grasped, you will realize how easy it is to dry plants successfully.

The many wonderful hours spent in pursuing this hobby led to my desire to share what I have learned with others and thus to the writing of this book. It is a "how to" book and is particularly intended for any homemaker who desires a source of practical, nontechnical information on collecting, drying and using dried plants. It should be of interest to anyone who takes pleasure in enhancing her home with artistic designs. It is not the kind of book you read through once and put on the shelf, but, like a cookbook, it should be kept within easy reach for reference.

For convenient use it is divided into three sections:

The first deals with plants to dry, what they are and where they can be found. The reader is given the widest possible choice since it discusses flowers, foliages, grasses, fruits, vegetables, cones, seed pods and wood, including those growing wild, in the garden and in the tropics. To try all the suggested plants would keep one occupied for years.

The second section concentrates on how to dry; there are step-by-step directions, assuming that the reader has no prior knowledge of the subject. Each example starts with basic principles, points out the techniques with emphasis on the practical approach and explains how the method is evolved from beginning to conclusion. Hundreds of specimens were dried, studied and compared with the aim of taking the guesswork out of drying by being specific as to the time for picking, the period required for drying and the method suited to various plants. The charts include much of this factual data.

The third section is devoted to the decorative uses for dried plants. There are ideas for the homemaker to make colorful decorations for the daily enjoyment of her family, for the hostess to create distinctive table pieces for her next party, and for the home decorator to make prints and plaques to adorn the walls of her home.

For the identification of plants, the primary authorities I have used are *Hortus* by L. H. Bailey and *The Practical Encyclopedia of Gardening* by Norman Taylor. As far as possible I have omitted technical terms from the text and used common or generally accepted names of plants. Scientific names are included in the identification charts.

It would be incorrect for me to claim that drying formulas were original or "my own," because the idea of using dried plants was conceived long before any of us were born. For example, skeletonizing of plants was developed to a high degree by the Chinese centuries ago. They not only skeletonized leaves, as we do today, but also flowers and seed pods. If you have an opportunity to visit the Cloisters in New York City, there you will see an authentic reproduction of how monks in medieval times dried their plants. You will find that the plants were bunched and suspended upside down, exactly as we do today.

My curiosity about preserving plants by drying started in my childhood when I gathered a few plants from the country for our city home. Dried plants were a part of our winter decorations but these bouquets would be sadly lacking in the light of present-day concepts of flower arrangement. From this random start over twenty years ago, drying plants has turned into a hobby of major interest. Not all of you will have my enthusiasm nor will your homes have pressed flowers in the telephone books, fruit and vegetables drying on the kitchen shelf or flowers dehydrating over the furnace, but I trust you will dry a few plants for artistic uses.

This book is for anyone interested in preserving the beauty in plants and throughout its pages you will find a new standard by which to evaluate dried plants. When you finish, I hope you will never speak of dried plants as dull dustcatchers but will think of them as colorful, artistic, lasting decorations. It is hard to find anything to surpass natural forms and colors for decorations.

Each year as the miracle of growth appears in Nature's world of plants much of the divine pattern of the universe is revealed to us as each leaf, flower and seed assumes its part in the plant world. Its color, shape and fragrance was created by a hand far greater and wiser than ours.

What and Where

1. A Fascinating Hobby

The instinct to decorate the home is as old as civilization itself and plant materials have always been the keynote of home decoration. Formerly freshly cut or growing plants were considered appropriate for home, club, office and window display but now dried plant materials are taking their place. The increasing popularity of this medium of artistic expression is a striking feature of the past ten years. It is not a passing fad or fancy; it is a permanent part of the decorative materials of this age.

American homes of today are planned with features which require plants as a part of their design and therefore plant materials are as necessary as curtains or rugs to complete an interior. Yet not more than two or three people out of a dozen use plants as an integral part of home design. If you think of the homes of friends which you have visited recently, can you recall many where dried plants were used as a permanent part of a room's decoration? A wise homemaker will find that dried plants offer

17

untold opportunities to beautify her home and that they are versatile enough to suit any style, old-fashioned, modern or contemporary. It is a wonderful sensation to walk into a room and discover an unusual or colorful arrangement of dried plants highlighting an interior.

No other part of home decoration is so much fun as choosing the right plants to dry and use for ornamentation in your rooms. You will find it is a fascinating hobby as well as a useful art. Time is a scarce item in any busy household schedule and a homemaker should welcome arrangements which will keep life and charm in a room for several weeks or months instead of a few days. Dried plants are economical since they can be used over and over again. For example, seed pods or leaves from the living-room arrangement will look new and fresh when rearranged in the hall or dining room. Certain tropical plants have stamina enough to endure for years. Between fall and spring, gardens are barren in many parts of our country and dried plants bridge this gap economically when the purchase of florist flowers would strain the budget. You will discover that having a supply on hand is as convenient as a supply of canned food on the pantry shelf. Arrangements can be made up in advance and stored until needed.

If you are one of those people who likes to sit by the fire in winter, dreaming of next year's garden as you visualize it from the seed catalog, it is a good policy to include plants which will serve a double purpose: bloom in the garden and flowers to dry. Another equally good idea is to grow plants whose color will harmonize with your furnishings.

Even if you live in a city apartment, it is possible to dry plants, because the process requires only a comparatively small area. Many florist flowers—Gladiolus, small Mums, Peonies, or Snapdragons—can be dried successfully. Perhaps the last time you received a box of flowers they were so lovely you hated to see them fade. If you had only realized it some of their beauty could have been preserved by drying.

The increasing enthusiasm for artistic arrangement of plants is a great modern trend. Women all over the nation have succumbed to its appeal and realize that tastefully assembled plant materials are essential to successful homemaking. It has become a nationwide hobby and is no longer limited to the members of garden clubs. You, as a homemaker, will find that pursuing this practical art can unlock the doors to new and fascinating fields. Once you learn to recognize the beauties of Nature a whole new world of adventure awaits you.

In the home there are many other uses for dried plants besides arrangements. In my area making prints with pressed, dried flowers is a popular project inspired by old-time flower prints. There is no limit to your imagination in making these pictures which preserve the beauty of summer under glass. Another form of expression with a modern feeling is the making of plaques. These wall decorations, which are made with dried plants, cover a wide variety in kind and style. Dried plants are festive enough for any occasion and have especially interesting uses in decorations for the Thanksgiving and Christmas holidays. Such decorations are fun to make and since they can be made far in advance of the busy season, save immeasurably on time at the last minute.

In any field of endeavor, progress demands new ideas and the decorative field is no exception. At present we are becoming aware of how many kinds of plants can be dried and the techniques, though developing rapidly, are open to improvement. As years go by it will prove interesting to see what progress is made since there is much more to be explored. The future depends on the ingenuity of the arranger, whether amateur or expert. Who knows but you may be one of those to add a new idea or technique?

2. What Dried Plants Are

Dried plants are those whose moisture or juice has been removed to assure that they will last indefinitely. The field is endless since you can include any kind of plant from weeds to those cultivated in a greenhouse. There are wonderful possibilities in parts of plants, such as a flower, a leaf, a seed pod, or a branch. When your attitude is flexible and your vision broad, you are able to dry things you never before dreamed you could.

In any explanation, the first step towards a clear understanding is to establish a few definite points as sources of reference. My definition for a dried plant is anything from the plant world which when dried retains three qualities: clear color, artistic shape, and decorative value. Anyone not familiar with the drying of plants may feel my interpretation is too liberal but a wide field must be drawn upon if any degree of originality is to be obtained. A discussion of the three points follows.

Color. The love of color is universal and color should be an outstanding consideration of any plant dried for decorative use. You may be amazed to find that the choice of color in dried plants is as wide as among fresh ones. Color can easily be retained in plants and when you take the trouble to process plants properly they will hold their color indefinitely.

In drying plants, color has always been my first concern because clear color adds life, zest and the dramatic quality which is such an important part of living plants. It balances out many another shortcoming. Since a great majority of plants tend to dry in a neutral tone, to retain color is especially desirable.

Nature gives to each of her plants a specific blend of color and all or a greater part of that color must be kept to give a dried plant the illusion of life. It would be hard to imagine Roses devoid of their soft pink colors or Delphiniums their variations of blue. The greatest compliment anyone can pay you is to ask how you have kept such colors in your plants when dry.

My displeasure becomes extreme when I hear a person say condescendingly that dried plants are colorless and uninteresting. It is amazing how many people still believe that brown and tan are the only colors possible! Today any color is possible in dried plants and there are as many as in fresh ones. The color wheel, Chart 1, names plants that dry in reds, yellows, blues, greens, oranges, violets and variations of these colors. Why not experiment with a few plants and see for yourself how much color can be retained when they are dry?

These are some of the better-known plant materials that you can dry for their color quality:

Red   Cockscomb, Peony, Pomegranate, Sumac, Zinnia.
Pink   Gladiolus, Larkspur, Peony, Snapdragon, Statice.
Yellow   Acacia, Goldenrod, Marigold, Strawflower, Yarrow, Zinnia.
Blue   Cornflower, Delphinium, Globe Thistle, Hydrangea, Larkspur.
Green   Foliage, Grasses, Seed Pods.
Orange   Bittersweet, Chinese Lantern Plant, Marigold, Strawflower, Zinnia.
Violet   Gladiolus, Heather, Lilac, Statice, Stock.

Gray, brown and tan are scarce colors in fresh plants and such earthy tones are often absolutely necessary to produce a desired result. Exotic seed pods and cones come within this range and native plants such as grasses or Dock have this same tonal quality.

These are some plant materials that can be dried for their neutral quality:

Gray   Artemisia, Bayberry, Dusty Miller.
Brown   Canna, Cones, Dock, Seed Pods, Traveler's-Tree.
Tan   Grasses, Leaves, Seed Pods, Wood Roses.
Black   Baptisia Pods, Magnolia Leaves, Teasel.
White   Everlasting, Honesty, Peony, Statice.

It is important to have color in dried plants no matter what use they are put to. Designs for prints and plaques are greatly enhanced by color. Colorful wood pieces are a boon to any decorator. Corsages must have color to be

festive and holiday decorations without it would be un-
thinkable. Even dried plants for food lose their appeal
without natural color.

Lighting and Color.   Color in dried plants is greatly
affected by artificial lighting. The flick of a switch can turn
a beautiful daylight color into a drab, lifeless one. The appeal of any color will depend on what type of lighting is
used. It may be incandescent or fluorescent, and it may be
direct or indirect in distribution.

The ordinary incandescent light is to some extent similar to daylight. Newer, soft pink types of lighting change
the appearance of everything in a room. Fluorescent-tube
light may create a warm or cool atmosphere depending on
the color type of the lamp. The color in dried plants improves when they are placed near or under lights and the
more intense the light, the better the color appears.

You can make the color of your dried plants more successful if you realize what changes occur. For the best results, keep in mind that yellow and orange plants are the
least affected by artificial light. Pink or red often assumes
a yellow cast, while blue and violet turn dull and dead-
ened. White changes little in any light. Oddly enough
the light values of most dried plants remain near their true
color at night.

Psychological Reaction to Color.   It is a well-recognized
fact that color has a psychological effect. When you choose
colors for dried plants, think of those which produce the
mood you want. Yellow, associated with sunshine, is exhil-

CHART 1. AROUND THE COLOR WHEEL
WITH DRIED PLANT MATERIALS

This variation of the standard color wheel adds plant names in the segments of the circle representing the colors of the spectrum. The plants included are intended as suggestions and are only a sampling of the hundreds of plants that will dry in color.

Yellow Range

Marigold   Daffodil
Gladiolus   Acacia
Yarrow   Zinnia
Chrysanthemum
Tansy   Tulip
Strawflower
Snapdragon
Goldenrod
Statice
Rose

Orange Range

Gourd
Zinnia
Marigold
Calendula
Strawflower
Bittersweet
Corn (ornamental)
Chinese Lantern Plant

Green Range

Ferns
Grasses
Hydrangea
Oak (leaves)
Beech (leaves)
Peony (leaves)
Milkweed Pods
Shallon (leaves)
Bells of Ireland
Magnolia (leaves)

Red Range

Gladiolus   Snapdragon
Celosia   Zinnia
Chrysanthemum
Peony   Stock
Pomegranate
Strawflower
Sumac   Tulip
Geranium
Petunia
Rose

Aster
Stock
Zinnia
Statice
Heather
Buddleia
Larkspur
Heliotrope
Strawflower
Lilac   Tulip
Globe Amaranth

Blue Range

Canterbury Bells
Globe Thistle
Salvia (Blue)
Delphinium
Cornflower
Hydrangea
Larkspur
Aster

Violet Range

arating, red and orange suggest warmth, green and blue denote coolness. Bright colors are stimulating and somber ones are depressing. No one can fail to realize that in winter brightly colored dried plants will give cheerfulness to a room when the landscape is dull and somber in color. Try your own reactions to a comparison of two dried plants, one in color and the other in a dull tone. You will naturally react with favor to the one in color.

Artistic Shape. What constitutes an artistic shape or form in a dried plant? It is any plant or part thereof which dries with lines suitable for decorative use. The lines can be straight, curved or irregular. The length and breadth of a shape determines its proportions and the thickness or thinness produces its third dimension and depth.

As you handle dried plants, their artistic shapes and forms are easier to recognize. For example; a Cattail or stalk of Mullein has a tall, cylindrical form. The Sweet Gum seed pods are perfect round balls, while a Lotus pod is cone-shaped. Seed cases grow in fascinating shapes. Some have long, slender lines like the Acacia and others twist and curl into circles or semicircles like the Locust.

Free forms are prevalent among plants and are easily identified in branches, leaves or roots of trees. Some are extremely graceful while others are enticingly angular.

The different physical features of flower heads provide another kind of artistic form. The large round form of a Peony, the cylindrical spike of a Gladiolus or the rounded crest of Cockscomb, are other examples. It is easy to imagine any number of ways to use their dominant shapes.

Leaves have a great variety of artistic shapes. There are long oval, small round, long narrow or clustered shapes. The Foliage Chart 5 on page 117 suggests many interesting leaves that are worthy of drying.

Decorative Value. Decorative value is difficult to express in words because it deals with the esthetic rather than the physical properties of a dried plant. However, when both color and artistic shape are inherent in a plant then this plant contributes decorative value to a design.

Any dried-plant decoration in your home is an expression of your personality. Individual likes and dislikes will influence the selection of any plant and a piece which is of interest to you may possess no allure for another. You have the greatest freedom of choice and no one else qualifies to dictate what type of plant contributes decorative value to your home. However, the décor of a home must be considered. You will learn that to have maximum decorative value, there must be a relationship between the dried plants and the architecture, walls and furnishings of a room. Designs of dried plants in arrangements, prints or plaques are as much a part of a room as its draperies.

There is a dried plant to suit each taste and interior, formal or informal. Formal furnishings usually lean toward antiques or fine reproductions of eighteenth- and nineteenth-century styles. Here designs of mass, reminiscent of the past era, have the greatest decorative value and add to the over-all atmosphere. In contemporary homes where casual living is the keynote, streamlined or naturalistic designs of dried plants are in perfect harmony.

3. Places to Look for Plants

Nature has covered a greater part of the earth's surface with plants and, to both the botanist and the layman, one of the most conspicuous features of the plant world is the endless variety in size and kind of its members. Some plants are microscopic in size while at the other extreme are the Redwood trees which grow hundreds of feet high. Another great difference among plants is in their span of life. Many wild and cultivated plants are annuals, living but a single season, some are biennials, living two seasons, and still others are perennials, growing for many years.

The average person thinks that plants consist of a few hundred varieties. But at the present time experts know of almost 340,000 distinct species of plants. Each has its own characteristics and habits of growth.

Wherever you may live, there are plants for drying, but they must be sought out and the possibilities of different kinds visualized. It is fun to search for exotic or foreign plants but we should learn to use the ordinary ones which grow in our own vicinity to the fullest advantage.

The places to look for materials to be dried can be divided into four general classes: Garden plants, Edible plants, Wild plants and Tropical and Unusual plants.

Garden Plants. The average garden, no matter what its size, provides valuable pieces that may be dried. Annuals like Marigolds and Zinnias, grown for quick floral returns, dry beautifully. At their season of maximum bloom you can pick an armful for drying without causing much loss of color in the flower beds. Ornamental trees and shrubs supply excellent foliage and a variety of interesting pods develop on garden plants. Some of these are Columbine, Iris and Peony. The plant is not harmed if a few of the seed pods are allowed to develop. See Chart 3, page 76, for other garden pods.

In a garden, there is something new to discover for drying at each season of the year. The same plant at intervals during its growing season may furnish quite different materials, such as bud, leaf, flower or seed pod. When they are stripped of petals the calyxes of many flowers dry and become another kind of material in your supply. It is a good idea to look over pieces while pruning for too often drying possibilities are tossed away.

Edible Plants. The fruit bins of markets everywhere have materials from which to choose for drying. Lemons, Limes, Tangerines, although normally thought of only as food, can be dried. Pomegranates are highly recommended

for their long-lasting quality. In winter, the top of a Pineapple is a reliable material to dry. I always keep the pits
of Avocado Pears and dry some with and without the
thin, dark skin. You will discover that many dehydrated
fruits, like Peaches, Apricots or Prunes, have interesting
forms and will supply an entirely different pattern for decorative uses.

Vegetables offer a number of attractive items for drying.
The seed clusters of Leeks or Onions have fascinating
shapes when dried and used in an arrangement. The leaves
of purple Cabbage, flowering Kale, Beet and Horse-Radish
all will retain color and form when they are dried. The
edible portion of Peppers, both red and green, and Okra
can be used. Artichokes and Corn are other edible plant
materials which can be dried and they are discussed in more
detail later.

Sugar Cane is another material that can be dried and
used for its unusual touch. Although this is a southern
product it is obtainable in the fruit markets of large cities.

Wild Plants.   Wherever you live, unusual and interesting plants grow wild in field, wood or meadow. When you
are alert and keep your eyes open, any trip or drive into
the country becomes a voyage of discovery.

During a summer excursion you will see Dock, Mullein
and Milkweed on the banks beside many roads while in
other areas you will find Thistle, Teasel and Tansy growing abundantly. Many kinds of wild flowers give color
to the countryside—Goldenrod brightens the scene from
Maine to Florida and Queen Anne's Lace carpets many

fields with white. Each provides a distinctive source for
dried materials.

The winter landscape has its own pleasing colors even
if they are more subdued than at any other time of the
year. A grayed twig, a gnarled branch, a weathered seed
pod or a cone has as much artistic value as a brightly
colored flower.

Conservation.   Many plants which are rare or rapidly
becoming extinct are protected by law. National and state
restrictions vary across the country but this need not seri-
ously affect the gathering of wild plants for there are
thousands that need no protection to survive. But never
should we be tempted to take a few pieces of protected
material and think that it does not matter. The Park Department or local Garden Club will gladly furnish you
with information on what plants are protected in your
area. It is a good policy to secure the list, learn to recognize
the plants included on it and persuade your friends to do
likewise.

When gathering wild plants do not trespass to pick the
the materials. The miles and miles of superb scenery on
the parkways must not be damaged nor the natural beauty
of public lands and parks. These are not the places to
search for plants, no matter how great the temptation
may be. Cutting or picking in any park is prohibited.

Tropical and Unusual Plants.   With modern means of
air transportation tropical and unusual plants—many with
exotic shapes and fascinating forms—are available at all

times of the year. Popular demand has led commercial firms to specialize in their shipment to florist markets from all parts of our country and the world.

The Hawaiian Islands, Florida and the West Coast supply us with many plants admirably suited to drying. Ti, easily available at the florist's, is the large, glossy green leaf from which the famous Hawaiian grass skirts are made. Florida's Palms supply many outstanding pieces that have dramatic qualities when dried. The Pacific region offers cones of many kinds and distinctive seed pods. These are but a few examples of plants for drying which are available through a supply house or florist.

A bit of personal history will illustrate the surprising ways that unusual plants come into one's possession. Who would ever suspect that the New York Botanical Gardens would be a likely source for obtaining materials to dry? We happened to be at the gardens on a day when they were trimming the Cactus greenhouse and had discarded a huge pile. The sight of such unusual material was a temptation no one could resist. We must have made an amusing picture picking Cactus from one end of the pile while a rubbish truck was doing the same at the opposite end. We were both racing at top speed to beat the other!

Picking and Drying

4. Drying Plants by Hanging

Even if we hate to think of winter during the abundant growth of spring and summer, these are the best times to gather the majority of plants for drying. Contrary to the popular misconception that drying plants for winter should be done in the fall, collecting and drying should be a year-round project—beginning in January and continuing right through the year.

The important thing in drying plants is to understand not only the drying processes but also the other factors which contribute to success. The growing habits of the plants will influence their drying quality. For example, Cactus, with its power to be self-sufficient, will take much longer to dry than a plant with a paper-thin petal structure like Statice or Strawflower.

The next factor is learning to know the proper time for cutting plants. There is, in the life of each plant, a time at which it is prime for cutting to dry. Generally, the best results are obtained by cutting flowers before they reach full maturity but not after color has begun to deteriorate. Because climate and weather differ from area to area, the actual moment of harvest can only be approximated. However, the stage in the growth of a plant which has proved best for cutting is covered as particular plants are discussed in this and subsequent chapters.

The third factor is the method of drying a plant. The basic principle of any drying process is the removal of moisture. Plants will not last indefinitely if they are only three-fourths dry but must be thoroughly devoid of moisture to keep satisfactorily. Methods are easy to learn and you will soon get the hang of it. The best way to gain information is to experiment by picking and drying plants using the various methods.

The majority of cultivated and wild plants can be dried by the simplest of all drying methods: hanging upside down. Through the years this technique of dehydration has been and still is the traditional way to dry plants. Our colonial ancestors used this method—old pictures show material neatly bunched and suspended over the kitchen mantel or from the rafters. Today, the tobacco industry employs this same principle for its valuable crop. Drying barns are a familiar sight in many parts of our country. The cut plants are hung upside down, and when the slat boards of the barn are open, the air circulates, evaporates the moisture and the leaves dry. This method of drying produces plants with form and color.

This chapter is devoted to a discussion of drying plants

by hanging upside down. Many of the same plants can be dried successfully in other ways also and this will be clarified as you read other chapters. The method you choose will depend on the use for which you are drying the plant. A flower or a leaf, dried in a dimensional form by hanging or with an agent, is appropriate for an arrangement, while the same kind may be pressed for a print. Regardless of how it is dried a plant should be kept as natural as possible in shape and color.

HANGING UPSIDE-DOWN METHOD

Gathering of Materials. Cut the plants on a bright sunny day and at the time in their growth when you feel the color is clear and true. This differs in various plants and specific examples are given later in the chapter. The length of stem is optional but for general use, in arrangements, 12″ to 15″ is suitable.

Preparation of Materials. Remove all unnecessary parts from the stem since the less there is on the stem, the faster it dries. This does not mean every stem must be stripped bare but use discretion as to how much can be safely left for drying.

Shaping of Materials. If a definite curve or line is desired, shape the plant while it is fresh. Once the shape is made, tie it securely and let the plant dry that way. After plants are dried it is difficult to reshape them with any degree of success.

Hanging of Materials. Group 3 or 4 stems into a small bunch and tie them together securely. As stems lose their moisture they shrink in size and unless tied securely often loosen enough to slip out. Elastic bands or Twistems are more effective than string to keep materials bound. Large stems like those of Cockscomb or thick stalks like those of Mullein should be hung singly.

Position of Hanging. Suspend the bunched materials or stalks upside down. This keeps the stems straight and the flower heads upright.

Means of Hanging. Plants may be suspended in any fashion that allows free passage of air to all surfaces. Hang bunches or stalks on a line as you would clothes on wash day or on a rack. (Illustrations 1, 2.) Less space is required if you attach 3 or 4 bunches to a wire coat hanger. Clip clothespins have proved excellent for attaching bunches to a line or hanger.

Space for Hanging. Use any warm, dry spot to hang plants provided it has free circulation of air; the cellar, attic, shed, garage or even the kitchen could be used. Plants should not be covered, shut up in a closet or exposed to direct sunlight while drying.

Time of Drying. In 8 or 10 days the majority of plants are dry but weather conditions at the time of drying will govern the number of days required. While they are drying, plants go through various stages of limpness. When completely dry, plants will be stiff to the touch and the stem snaps easily.

Storage of Materials. Remove the bunches or stalks when they are dry and store in a covered box. Several florist boxes will hold enough to supply the average person's needs.

HOW TO MAKE A DRYING RACK

A drying rack is extremely useful in the air-drying of plants by hanging upside down. It is easy to make a rack

Robert Scharff

1. CIRCULAR DRYING RACK

2. RECTANGULAR DRYING RACK

and anyone handy with tools can construct one with little time or expense. A rack should be of lightweight wood, for easy moving from place to place. The following specifications were used for the racks shown in Illustrations 1 and 2.

The rectangular rack is 2' wide, 4' long and 3' high. It was made with "parting strips" ½" by ¾" with all joints doweled and glued. The 4 crosspieces, plus the edge strips, provide ample room to hang many plants at the same time and still have free circulation of air. The frame was finished with maple stain.

Two drying screens were made to fit on top of the rectangular rack. Each screen is 2′ square and of the same strips and finish as the rack. The short 5½″ legs are notched so that they hold and rest on the rack. The netting of the screen is Fiberglas. Each screen is removable for use both on the rack and separately.

The circular rack for drying was fashioned from the base of a standing lamp and a pole 38″ long and 1⅝″ in diameter. The ¼″ dowel pins are 36″ long and radiate at equally spaced angles through the pole. Several coats of white paint add a finish and protect the wood.

WILD PLANTS

There are myriads of lovely and beautiful wild plants which can be dried. In picking wild plants, if you take a few simple precautions, the countryside will be kept beautiful and wild plants will be perpetuated. The conservation restrictions on rare or rapidly disappearing native plants were mentioned in Chapter 3, and such plants should not be cut for drying.

Just because a plant is growing wild, there is no reason to destroy it. You should never rip it up by its roots or tear off a branch or blossom at random to obtain decorative material. The plant will continue its normal growth if you sever only the decorative portion, with a clean, clear cut, as you do in your own garden. If you take the time to shake loose seeds onto the ground, next year another plant will bloom. In gathering wild materials everyone should learn to pick a sensible amount and resist the temptation to bring home an armful.

Precaution! In gathering wild plants you should remember that many are poisonous. It is usually only the leaf which is dangerous to the touch but in some cases roots, stems, flowers, berries, juice or bark are equally poisonous. The worst offenders are the poisonous Ivy, Sumac and Oak.

Wild Flowering Plants. Wild flowering plants are not as sturdy as cultivated ones and success in drying them depends on proper cutting and treatment immediately. Wild flowers should be cut before they become mature and, as they wilt quickly, should be carried home in a box or plastic bag. The stems should be recut, unnecessary foliage removed and the stems put into water for several hours. When revived and crisp, they are bunched and hung. Some of the better-known wild flowers which can be dried successfully follow.

Bergamot is an attractive aromatic plant and its tall stem with lavender or rose whorl flower is conspicuous during summer and fall. Since all the florets in the dense head do not open at the same time, you may prefer to dry the honeycomb center without the florets.

Black-Eyed Susan with its bright, golden-rayed petals and cone-shaped dark center brightens the fields from June to September. It is a good wildling to use for drying if it is cut when the petals are curved inwards—never drooping. Foliage may remain on the stem.

Butterfly Weed with a large, brilliant rounded cluster attracts attention when in bloom. It can be dried by hanging or in an agent.

3. WILD PLANTS

1. Grain   2. Field Grasses   3. Dock   4. Cattail   5. Millet
6. Goldenrod   7. Sumac   8. Butterfly Weed   9. Teasel
10. Mullein   11. Pearly Everlasting   12. Teasel   13. Yarrow   14. Moth Mullein   15. Tansy   16. Marsh Grass
17. Milkweed   18. Sumac.

Daisy, Field or Oxeye is a common sight in fields throughout the United States. The flower, composed of a yellow center surrounded by white petals, can be dried by hanging or in an agent.

Pearly Everlasting is valuable for drying. The flower, composed of flattened clusters of tiny heads with prominent white bracts, must be cut when half open to remain white. Six or 8 of the thin stems may be allowed to a bunch.

Goldenrod is among the most colorful of wild flowers with a long flowering season and many varieties from which to choose. If cut while still in bud, it will open when dry.

Joe-Pye Weed often called Boneset, is a handsome plant which has been growing in the meadows since the days of the Indians. Its name commemorates a medicine man who used it as one of his cures. It is cut when the florets in the large heads are dark and practically in bud. Full-blown heads dry dull in color.

Tansy, another of the wild aromatic plants, has become naturalized over portions of the United States. Its tight clusters of small button-like florets should be cut when a brilliant yellow. During drying their size shrinks somewhat but the color remains.

Thistle, Common, Spear or Bull, is well known for its spiny leaves and red-lavender flowers. If during drying the color in its thin petals fades, they may be pulled out of the case leaving an attractive form with a soft-textured lining.

Queen Anne's Lace, Wild Carrot, is an exquisite weed with a large, flat, dainty, white head. To have the flower remain white, it should be cut when not more than three-fourths open. Flowers may be dried by hanging, in an agent or by pressing. Try a few buds and some of its fine foliage for variety.

Yarrow has an extremely pungent odor in both its foliage and flower. From June to October its flat, white or yellow heads on tough, erect stems are a common sight along the roadside. The white heads are excellent for massed bouquets.

Other Wild Plants. You need never come home empty-handed from a drive since interesting pieces for drying may be collected almost everywhere. In gathering seed pods or foliages, spread them out in a single layer, preferably on paper. Packing them in a carton or basket with paper between each layer is an excellent idea for the trip home until you can process them. If you toss your find carelessly into the car you will regret it, since a wilted flower or broken stem may destroy a piece that is hard to replace.

GRASSES

Each section of our country has its own native species of grasses and the variety is endless. Lovely grasses can be gathered in field, meadow or marsh and along the roadside. Each type has a distinctive character and the ornamental rather than horticultural quality influences the choice for decorative use. If the eye is quick enough to see it, one type will be perfect for a mixed arrangement while another will provide the right curve or height for a design outline. The charming forms of wild grasses have many uses in arrangements, pictures and plaques.

In spring and early summer, wild grasses have lacy, graceful patterns and soft green color, and if they are picked within 2 weeks of their development these features are retained. However, if the same grasses grow until fall the resulting color will be a neutral tan, buff or fawn. Each year all of my wild grasses are gathered and dried by the Fourth of July. The Reed or Plume types of marsh grasses are cut in early fall when their heads are rich in color.

Grasses are often included in gardens because of their striking foliage and feathery flower clusters. Bamboo and Pampas types are grown for their handsome, towering height, and Plume and Cloud for their rose or purple heads. Such grasses are cut for drying when about half developed. Rabbit's-Tail grass has a most attractive soft white tail and is cut during the summer as it matures. The graceful sweep in the drooping panicles of Sea Oat is unusual and this grass dries in a lovely shade of tan though its beauty is often spoiled by artificial coloring.

Grasses are hung upside down to dry in bunches of not more than 6, (larger ones—not more than 4). Stems of grasses are weak and hanging stiffens the stems and straightens the heads. Grasses fluff up and become larger in size when dry. If you want the stem and head to curve stand them in an empty vase, allowing plenty of space around each one for air circulation, and the weight of the head will curve the stem. Choose a dry, cool, shaded spot for hanging—direct sunlight or extreme heat gives grasses the texture of hay. Frequently when grasses are cut they have already begun to dry and will process quickly. Once dried, grasses should be handled carefully and stored with tissue paper in a long box.

GRAINS

Of the 3,500 useful food-producing species of grains, the best known are Barley, Corn, Oats, Rice, Rye and Wheat, and all are ideally suited to decorative work.

Grains for decorative uses are picked when they are at the green stage in their growth. Grains dried then will remain closely wrapped in their case and the case, with its grain inside, is far more attractive than when it is empty. Grains are bunched and hung upside down.

Corn, truly an American plant, has been well known since the days of the Indians. Today it grows in many sizes from dwarf Popcorn to the 20′ plants of the Middle Western states. Several parts of a Corn plant can be dried for decorative use. If the leaves are picked when colorful, they dry in green, red-brown and tan tones. Dry Corn tassels are like a fluffy grass. Stalks are always used for harvest decorations and may be cut into suitably sized lengths, either before or after drying. Ears, with colorful kernels, are a traditional symbol for fall and Thanksgiving use. Various kinds come in distinctive colors, such as Calico, Rainbow, Variegated, Golden and Popcorn. If the color of the kernels is especially choice, here is a tip on how to keep such ears. Store them in a sealable container, such as a tin box, and add a handful of moth crystals to prevent insect damage. Corn will keep a beautiful, clear color for several years this way.

GOURDS

The Gourd family has a great diversity of form, size and color in its peculiar fruit. These summer vines are vigorous climbers and their fruits come under two general types, the small ornamental gourds and the larger hard-shelled gourds. The small ones are the more colorful and are adaptable to many decorative uses. They grow in bicolors, stripes and solid colors. The commonly recommended method for harvesting these small gourds is to pick them after the first frost, but I have found that small gourds dry better if they are picked as they mature throughout the season. In the fall, many gourds will be too ripe to keep. Only fully mature, but not overly ripened gourds, will dry in good color. The stem of a mature gourd is dry and fingernail pressure will leave no impression on the outer covering of the fruit. The large hard-shelled gourds require a longer growing season to reach maturity than the smaller kinds and in colder climates they are not harvested until after frost has killed the vines. The large gourds grow in quaint and unusual shapes.

Method for Drying Gourds.   A gourd is cut with a stem of several inches and all dust or garden dirt is removed from its surface with soap and water. Care should be exercised not to damage the outer skin during the washing for such mishandling impairs its drying and keeping quality.

To assure good keeping, the gourd is immersed in a household disinfectant solution before being hung to dry. Also prick a tiny hole in each end of the gourd with a small sharp point about the size of a hatpin, for ventilation during drying.

Attach a string to the stem of either large or small gourds and hang singly in a cool place until dry. Gourds require several months to dry and the larger they are, the more time they take. Shake the gourd and if the seeds rattle it is dry, if not it requires more time.

If the stems of some gourds are not long enough to attach strings, they may also be dried by laying them on a raised, perforated surface, in a cool spot. A rack for cooling cakes is an excellent raised platform on which to dry gourds, allowing a free circulation of air to all surfaces. Turning the gourd several times during drying hastens the process.

Any film or mold which forms on the gourd during drying can easily be removed with soap and water. After washing, dry gourds again for several days before applying a finish. It is only fair to warn that there will be a few casualties. Out of a dozen gourds, 8 or 9 successfully dried is a good percentage.

The surface pattern of many dried gourds is beautiful and needs no added finish to be decorative. Small white ones dry with a lovely cream or ivory tone. Shellac or varnish gives a glossy finish while floor wax produces a duller, smooth effect. Paint will make a gourd any color you wish.

Gourds which are purchased at a store often have been given a coating of lacquer, before they have had a chance to dry. The moisture in the gourd cannot escape through this coating and such gourds show signs of deterioration within a few weeks. If you do not grow gourds, the best plan is to purchase them from a grower. He displays them as they come from his vines and you can cure and treat them properly. To make gourds last indefinitely, thorough drying is absolutely necessary.

FRUITS AND VEGETABLES

Dried citrus fruits, such as Lemon, Lime, Orange and Tangerine, are entirely different from other dried plants. They may be dried in the same fashion as gourds, by laying them on a rack, in a cool dry spot.

At the market, when selecting fruits, pick out those which are firm, not overly ripe, and free of marks or blemishes. Wash and dry the fruit before laying it on the rack; no disinfectant is necessary. Sometimes, within the first week or 10 days, the fruit may get a little soft and unless you have had previous experience you are apt to discard it as worthless. The fruit will begin to harden within a couple of weeks and after a month become dry and firm. Citrus fruits require no finish because the skin turns reddish brown and acquires the texture of rough paper.

Pomegranates are wonderful for drying because they retain their vivid color. They are dried on a rack like citrus fruits, but it may take 3 months for a Pomegranate to become firm and dry. They may shrink a little in size but this only makes them more attractive. They will add a splash of color to any dried-plant grouping.

Among vegetable leaves suitable for drying are green and purple Cabbage, Flowering Kale, Beet and Horse-Radish. Whichever you select, the leaves should be cut when in their prime of color and freshness. Hang the leaves upside down in groups.

Equally important from the vegetable garden are seed stalks of Onion and Leek. Each has a fascinating formation of tall stalks with clusters of seeds at the top. They should be cut before the seeds begin to drop and hung individually. If you wish some definite curve or angle in the long stem, you can manipulate it while fresh, and dry it that way. The flower cluster of Rhubarb may also be dried, if cut before in full flower.

Globe or French Artichokes are handsome vegetables to dry. Originally, they were native to the Mediterranean area but today we grow thousands of acres, mainly in California, for food. The edible flower heads have scales tightly closed when you purchase them but after a few days in a warm room, they can be easily opened and pressed apart. This is done to speed drying the thick solid heads and to form a fascinating, rounded flower form. The scales spring back during drying and should be repeatedly opened to keep the desired shape. Inserting face tissues between the scales keeps them apart during drying. The stem of the artichoke is short and stubby and if a small stick is forced into the stem while fresh and allowed to remain, the head is easier to use. Artichokes are hung in a cool, airy place to dry. Mention is made of their uses in Section 3 of this book.

BERRIES

Brilliant berries give many plants a dramatic touch but because of their fleshy structure only a few kinds dry successfully. The colorful berries of Fire Thorn, Snowberry, Russian Olive, and Coralberry, will not dry or last indefinitely, even when the stems are kept in water. The colorful berries of Viburnum are not suitable for drying and Beauty-Berry loses almost all of its glorious violet when dry.

The following berries have been dried successfully:

Pepper Tree grows in various climates and its masses of rose-colored berries are wonderful for drying and they last for years. The stem is cut when the color in the berries is brilliant. All the leaves are removed and each stem is hung singly for several weeks.

Bayberry is a bushy plant whose small, dark-green leaves exude a lovely spicy fragrance when crushed between the fingers. In the fall, groups of small, gray berries appear under the leaves in cascades all along the stems of the plant, and their waxy film makes them excellent for drying. In the late fall or at the time of the first frost the stems are cut. The upper part of the stem bearing the leaves is entirely cut off and the remaining stem of berries is hung for about 2 weeks to dry. These are the berries that have been used since colonial days for making Bayberry candles.

Sumac is a riot of color in fall. The Staghorn variety is the largest and the most common of harmless sumacs. It may be recognized by its antler-shaped branches topped by dense, cone-shaped clusters of berries. They may be as long as 8″ and range in color from red-orange to maroon. If the stem is cut when the berries are brilliant, they hold color when dry. The leaves are removed before each stem is hung upside down, for about a week. Smooth Sumac is a smaller plant but its smaller cluster of berries is as colorful. Staghorn, Smooth, Fragrant and Shining are some of the safe, nonpoisonous sumacs which may be handled without fear. Fortunately, Poisonous Sumac is limited to swamps and bogs. The yellowish-white drooping berries are much like those of the Poison Ivy.

Bittersweet, a vigorous plant, climbs and twists itself about the nearest fence or tree. In late fall, it bursts into full beauty as the husks open and show their bright orange seeds within. If it is picked when the husks are green and unopened, the color is better. After several days of indoor drying the husks will open and expose the seeds. In this way the husks remain on the berries all through the winter, but if the husks had opened out-of-doors, they would drop easily when handled.

CACTUS

Cactus comes in a variety of shapes, sizes and colors, many of which are good for drying. In the colder northern climates, few Cacti are hardy enough to grow out of doors but in warmer areas they flourish in the garden. Cacti are constructed to adapt themselves to drought or adverse conditions by their ability to store moisture. This characteristic causes some pieces to take as long as 3 or 4 months to become absolutely dry. Large pieces of cactus are hung singly, while 2 or 3 small pieces may be bunched together. Once a cactus is dry it lasts for years and is strong enough to be washed without damaging the condition of the material.

The placement of spines or thorns is a distinguishing mark of cactus. When the larger forms are dry the spines become prominent and create an extremely interesting pattern. These spines are stiff and sharp-pointed so that extra care and protection for the hands is necessary in handling them.

HERBS

There is an increasing interest in culinary herbs and the modern housewife finds that a few of these growing in her garden or on the window sill can be a practical help in cooking. Many of the herbs that we use today have a long history. Such herbs as Sage, Thyme, Dill, Rosemary and Mint were brought to this country by the Pilgrims. The food market can furnish any kind of herb in a neat package but those which are grown and prepared at home are more exciting.

The ideal time to cut herbs for drying is on a clear day when the sun is not hot and there is no dew on the plant. Herbs to be dried for the leaf only are gathered before the flower opens and any damaged leaves are removed before drying. For example, in Mint the greatest amount of aromatic oil is in the leaf before the bloom appears. In harvesting herbs for their seeds, like Dill, it is best to gather them before they begin to drop the seed and so avoid unnecessary loss.

Herbs may be cut more than once during a season as the second growth has the same quality for drying. Annual herbs can be cut severely but the future growth of perennials may be impaired if more than a third of the plant is cut.

Culinary herbs can be dried by screening or by hanging.

Screening. Immediately after cutting, the stem with leaves is placed on a mesh screen in a warm spot and left until it is dry. The process is hastened if the stems are turned several times. If more than one kind is processed at the same time, labels will avoid confusion when they are dry.

Hanging.   Bunch 3 or 4 stems of leaves and hang upside down in a warm place until they are dry. To retain maximum flavor it is advisable to dry herbs in a shaded spot; never in sunlight or complete darkness. Stems of herbs dried in this way are suitable for arrangements.

With either of the above drying methods, weather conditions will determine the processing time. In good weather herbs dry in 5 or 6 days but during a damp spell may take longer. Herbs are dry when the stem can be snapped and broken easily. Flavor will be lost if herbs are dried longer than necessary.

Preparation and Storage for culinary purposes.   Leaves are stripped from the stem and may be stored whole or rubbed through a sieve. In the past, it was customary to grind herbs in a mortar but a sieve is easier.

Usually each herb is kept separately and stored in an individual air-tight jar. Small glass apothecary jars have served my needs and half a dozen on a shelf near the stove will be adequate for a family.

To the gourmet herbs are as necessary as salt and pepper. A new taste is always a welcome change and each herb that is grown and dried will provide that extra something for a savory dish.

Fragrant Materials.   While you are drying herbs for culinary purposes it is a good idea to gather a few sweet-scented materials for a potpourri or a sachet. Since the days of Greece and Rome the potpourri has been a way to retain fragrance in dried materials. The habit of gathering and drying scented petals for a sachet has been handed down from generation to generation. Today the custom is again in use by those who prefer garden fragrance to artificial scents.

For centuries Rose petals have been used for the potpourri or sachet because they hold their fragrance satisfactorily. They are so widely used that drug-supply firms import commercially dried rose petals. The petals of other fragrant flowers, like Carnations, Geraniums, Heliotrope, Honeysuckle, Lavender, Lilacs and Spice Pinks, are also adequate. During the summer season many kinds of flowers can supply petals for drying and what you use will depend upon your taste and the scent you prefer. Leaves dried for this purpose should be the mildly fragrant ones like Mint or Rosemary and not those which will overpower the delicate odor of the other petals.

The fragrant full-blown flowers which are used for drying should be cut on a clear day in the late afternoon. As only the petals are used, the stem of a flower may be cut quite short. The stem of a cut flower is placed in a small amount of water and left until the next day when the flowers are dismembered. Then only the petals are spread on absorbent paper in a warm spot but never in sunlight. If the petals are shuffled daily they should be completely dry in 4 to 5 days. Leaves are processed separately and dried in the same way. As petals shrink when they are dry it may be necessary to process several batches to have a sufficient quantity for a potpourri or sachet. If you dry a few petals for their color, such as Cornflower, Delphinium, Peony or Zinnia, it will make the final mixture more alluring. Dried petals or leaves may be kept in a covered container until used if they are lightly sprinkled with salt.

One of the most interesting features of a potpourri is the container. It should be ornamental, sturdy and have a fitted cover. If you are fortunate enough to have an old rose jar, it is a perfect container. Today with the great revival of interest in apothecary jars as accessories, they can be obtained in many varieties.

Of the many ways to prepare a potpourri mixture, the following is a good simplified method. After a quantity of petals are dried, begin by placing a layer in the jar. These are sprinkled with salt and a combination of Orrisroot, spices and brown sugar. Use 1 ounce of Orrisroot, 1 ounce of brown sugar and 1 ounce of powdered spices to each quart of dried petals. The Orrisroot, which serves as a fixative for the petals, can be obtained at the drugstore. The spices, selected according to personal preference, could be Allspice, Cinnamon, Cloves, Mace or Nutmeg. Some people add bits of dried Orange or Lemon rind or a small quantity of oil of roses. The process is continued by placing another layer of petals, sprinkling them and then repeating layer by layer until the jar is filled. Stir and mix thoroughly and then cover the jar. The mixture is allowed to age for 3 weeks and during this time it should be stirred twice weekly to blend the ingredients. Once blended, the fragrance will last for years and every time you remove the cover of the jar a pleasing odor will remind you of your summer garden.

It is fun to make a sachet for the closet, drawer or linen closet. Petals and leaves are selected and dried as described above. The making of a sachet is very simple. The dried petals and leaves are mixed according to choice and inserted in a small case made of a porous fabric. Lavender is inevitably associated with sachets but there are all sorts of other combinations possible, such as equal quantities of Carnation and Spice Pink petals with Rose Geranium leaves, and a few Cornflower petals for color. Other pleasing combinations are Rose petals with Mint blossoms or Rose Geraniums with Geraniums. Properly dried materials will hold their fragrance for several years.

The pomander ball is another form of dried fragrance. The short stems of whole Cloves are pressed firmly into the skin of a fresh Orange until it is thickly and entirely covered—an ounce of whole Cloves is sufficient. Then a small quantity of powdered Cinnamon is placed in a bag (paper or plastic) and the Orange studded with Cloves is gently shaken in the bag until it is well coated. The Orange is removed from the bag and placed in a dry, dark spot for 10 days. During that time it becomes a firm, fragrant ball which will keep its spicy odor indefinitely. The pomander ball is tied around each way with a length of brightly colored ribbon and attached to a hook or coat hanger. This is one of our family favorites for a closet sachet. Several of these balls make a spicy accessory for a dried arrangement or a fruit composition.

5. Seed Pods, Cones and Nuts

Nature provides many plants with a distinctive pod or case to protect and dispense their seed. Each pod or case is an ingenious creation and these specialized structures are adaptable for decorations to great advantage. Seed pods, cones and nuts have a similar mission in Nature's scheme of perpetuation and therefore are discussed under one chapter heading.

SEED PODS

Gathering. Since seeds mature at various times of year, pods for drying are gathered accordingly. The seed pod, for maximum effectiveness, is picked at that time in its growth when its size, form and color are adaptable to decorative use. For example, the seed cases of the Columbine or Siberian Iris are better in dried color if they are picked while still green and closed, while a Honey Locust pod should remain on the plant until it turns a rich chocolate brown. The time of harvesting will determine the color of a pod when it is dried.

Drying. Pods which grow on a long stem, along a stalk, or clustered on a main stem can be dried by hanging as described in Chapter 4. Small, short-stemmed pods can be dried in single layers, either on a flat surface or in an open box, in a warm dry place. The process can be hastened if they are turned over at 1- or 2-day intervals. The drying time varies with the size, thickness and texture of a pod. You will soon learn to tell when a pod is fully dried. It will be stiff, firm to the touch and tissues will appear woody. When pods open naturally on a plant, they require little drying. The majority of pods last much longer if the seeds are removed before drying; however, if you prefer to keep the seeds in their cases, they too can be dried successfully. Such pods are particularly attractive when the case and seeds are of different colors.

Tree Pods. Trees have numerous kinds, sizes and shapes of pods or cases for their seeds and a few for drying are mentioned below:

BEAN-SHAPED PODS

Black Locust has a pod 3″ to 4″ long. The outside is dark brown, the inside is white.

Honey Locust pods can be as long as 16″. They twist and curl into fascinating, glossy brown shapes.

Catalpa pods grow up to 18″ and these pencil-thin, dark brown formations can be seen clinging to the tree's winter profile.

Robert Scharff

4. TREE SEED PODS

1. Eucalyptus 2. Catalpa 3. Honey Locust 4. Woman's-Tongue Tree 5. Mimosa 6. Sweet Gum 7. Sycamore 8. Sterculia 9. Ailanthus 10. Black Locust 11. Magnolia.

Acacia pods grow up to 10". In most varieties, the pods curl and pass through color changes. If they are picked before maturity, they will remain green when they are dried.

Poinciana pods are giants of 20", and when split, the interesting pattern of indentations for the seed is light in color.

BALL-SHAPED CASES

Sweet Gum has a 1"-round, thorny capsule whose many cavities end in harmless spines. These balls are tough and cling to the tree's branches long after the brilliant fall foliage has disappeared.

Sycamore (Buttonwood) has a 1" globular-shaped seed case which dangles from a thin stem among the upper branches. Some grow singly, others in twos or threes. They are tan in color and soft to the touch.

CLUSTER PODS

Ailanthus (Tree of Heaven) has brilliant clusters of red-orange seed pods. The small pods in the clusters are shaped like airplane propellers with a tiny seed in the middle. If picked in their red-orange stage this color remains when they are dried.

Red Gum (Eucalyptus) has a curious upright cluster of bell-shaped seed cases with a hole in the flat top. Because of their shape, the florist refers to them as "Bell Pods."

Jacaranda grows in the warmer parts of the country. It has one of the most intriguing seed clusters. The blue flowers turn into unique squashed pods like small clamshells. The outside is green-brown with the roughness of a tree bark and the inside is light cream and satiny.

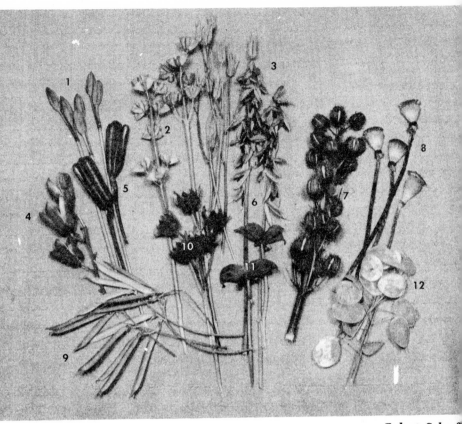

5. GARDEN SEED PODS

1. Siberian Iris 2. Gas Plant 3. Columbine 4. Yucca
5. Lily 6. Plantain Lily 7. Castor-Oil Plant 8. Poppy
9. Perennial Sweet Pea 10. Rose of Sharon 11. Peony
12. Honesty.

Sterculia, a warm-climate tree, has a cluster of picturesque oblong brown pods. Each of the pods has a point at both ends and grows in an upright position. As they dry, the case splits open to expose several rows of small golden-yellow seeds.

Paulownia has conspicuous large purple flowers and unusual oval brown seed pods which hang in clusters like grapes. These remain on the tree all through the winter.

Garden Pods. In a garden, annuals, perennials, bulbs and shrubs develop attractive seed formations and the following are a few suitable for drying:

BALL-SHAPED

Globe Thistle has a spiny ball-shaped case which remains blue when it is dry.

Chinese Lantern Plant has balloon-shaped pods ranging along its stiff stem. They are a brilliant orange and will remain so if they are cut when the color is bright, foliage stripped from the stem and hung. These shapes can be converted into orange flowers by cutting the ridges in the formation into petals and allowing them to curl about the large, dark seed in the center.

FLOWER-SHAPED

Gas Plant has many attractive, dainty tan seed cases on long stems.

Rose of Sharon develops dark brown flower-shaped cases on its branches.

Peony has an unusual seed case. As the case develops and opens naturally the sections in the pod become the petals of a flower.

SPIKES OF PODS

Hosta has an inconspicuous flower which develops into an interesting spike of small seed cases.

Delphinium and Larkspur have stems with small 3-chambered cup-shaped cases.

Snapdragon seed vessels are small, fat and spaced beautifully on the stem.

BEAN-SHAPED

Wisteria, a popular ornamental vine tree, has oblong, fat, soft-green pods with a fuzzy downy exterior which remains after drying.

Perennial Sweet Pea has a pod as attractive as its flower and if picked for drying when green will remain so.

Trumpet Vine or Creeper is highly ornamental with its clusters of red-orange trumpet-shaped flowers. A delightful satiny-smooth dark brown bean-shaped pod about 5″ long develops after the flower fades.

OVAL-SHAPED

Oriental Poppy has an oval cup-shaped seed pod with a ribbed lid to protect the small black seeds. Each pod rests atop a long slender stem.

Tulip flowers have oval three-sectioned light-tan seed cases.

Members of the Lily family produce interesting seed vessels. Iris, especially Siberian, yields useful pods and can be dried in several shades from tan to dark brown if they are cut at intervals in their development.

Wild Pods.   The wayside, field and meadow abound in plants which bear interesting cases for their seed. Obviously there are a great many more than those mentioned below:

SPIKE

Mullein, the common name for wild Verbascum, grows to be 6' in height and the greater part of the stalk is covered with small seed cases. The later the stalk is cut, the darker it will dry. Like all thick-stemmed plants, each stalk should be hung singly during drying. The straight spike is not always adaptable to use, therefore while fresh, it may be molded into a curve.

Cattails, a popular swamp plant, are often referred to as Reeds. They will last for years if picked early and immediately dipped in shellac. The shellac penetrating the absorbent tufts, holds them firm, yet does not mar the soft outward appearance. Drying is completed by hanging for 8 to 10 days.

CLUSTER

Milkweed pods are a masterpiece of packaging. When the flat seam on the bumpy exterior of a pod is slit, it reveals how expertly each seed is packed, one overlapping another and equipped with a downy tuft. When pods are picked while green and the seed removed, the case dries green, but if they open naturally on the plant, their color when dry is tan. Milkweed should be gathered conservatively because according to entomologists, the Monarch Butterfly uses it exclusively for breeding.

PRICKLY

Teasel has a long spiky stem and a prickly thick head. When picked in summer the seed head remains green, in fall it dries tan and those wintering in the open dry black. Since colonial days Teasel has been used in textile manufacture to raise the nap on woolen cloth.

FLOWER-SHAPED

Sneezeweed with its yellow flowers is colorful in fall. When the petals fade the center brown disks become attractive flower-shaped seed cases.

Wild Bergamot with its tall stem and lavender flower is well known. In fall its seed cases look like miniature brown pin-cushion flowers.

STEM

Dock, often called Sorrel, is a common roadside plant and is one of the easiest to dry. By picking the stem of tiny seeds at various intervals in its growing season the color can range from green in spring to chocolate brown in fall. The copper tones of midsummer are a joy to any arranger. Remove all the tiny leaves between the seeds and the larger ones on the stems. Hang 2 stalks together and they will dry in several days.

Unusual Pods. The word unusual is applied to the following pods since they are odd, quaint, or picturesque in appearance when compared to other better-known kinds.

Traveler's-Tree has a trunk like that of a palm and tremendous leaves which resemble those on a Banana Tree, radiating from the trunk like ribs in a fan. The cluster of pods which grows at the base of the fan is composed of a number of small pods. When dry, each one splits open, revealing many small, fuzzy, turquoise-blue seeds. This color is in striking contrast to the dark brown of the fibrous exterior of the pod.

There is an interesting legend connected with the name of

this tree. In olden days, a forest traveler rejoiced to discover one of the trees: he could find his way because the leaves always grow from east to west and could quench his thirst because the flower bracts and leaf stalks hold a small quantity of water. The tree was a friend, hence the name.

Screw Bean (Tornillo) has a curious pod. Each cluster is composed of 4 or 5 thin, glossy light-tan pods, about 1″ long and twisted tightly round and round like a corkscrew.

Wood Roses have one of the loveliest of all seed cases. This tropical plant of the Morning-Glory family is also referred to as Spanish Arbor Vine, Ceylon Morning-Glory and Frozen Roses. The case, the size of a rose, has a woody texture and half-open petals that curl about a large seed ball in the center. The outer surface is cocoa brown and the inner a creamy tan. Though these cases appear to be fragile, with care they will last for years.

Lotus has a fascinating seed case which can be likened to a foreshortened inverted cone, about 4″ in diameter and 2″ deep. The top is flat, has a wavy edge and numerous deep-pitted holes, each containing a large seed. The color when dried is cocoa brown and the texture dull and smooth.

The massive flower and enormous blue-green leaves of the Lotus are spectacular. It was a favorite of ancient peoples and one of the first plant materials to appear in decorations.

Wiliwili is a tree native to Hawaii. The flowers are orange and when the cluster of narrow curling pods opens there are scarlet seeds within.

CONES

Conifer is the horticultural term for trees which have narrow needlelike leaves and bear their seeds in woody cones. A few of the better-known conifers are Pine, Fir, Spruce, Cedar, Hemlock and Redwood.

Cones are one of my favorite materials for drying since their forms differ so extensively and harmonize so readily with other kinds of dried plants. They have inspired modern designers to adapt their form to motifs for china, fabric and wallpaper. Many people use cones only during the Christmas season but they should be considered for use the rest of the year.

The decorative value of cones is in the distinctive formation of the structure and the effective ways the wood disks or scales, on which the naked seeds lie, are placed. If you compare a half dozen different kinds of cones you will realize how great is their variety in shape, size and structure. The scales in a cone remain tightly folded while the seed is ripening, but with maturity they swing open to dispel the seed, thus often doubling the size of a cone.

The color of a cone is important for ornamental use and though the tones of brown do predominate, there are red-brown, green-brown, light and dark brown and all shades of tan. Spanish Fir cones have a deep violet hue while those of the Pinyon Pine have chartreuse and yellow highlights.

Treatment of Cones. Cones gathered in their natural habitat require treatment before they are ready for decorative uses. On the scales of many cones is a sticky substance known as pitch and anyone who has ever picked up cones knows how gummy this can be. A shampoo in detergent suds, aided by a stiff brush on the stubborn spots, will

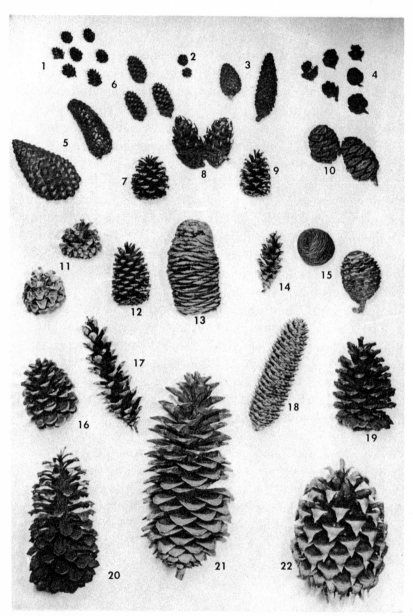

Robert Scharff

remedy this. Cones purchased from the florist are usually clean and ready for use.

Drying of Cones.   Cones may be dried by natural or artificial heat. In summer they may be spread out-of-doors on a flat surface for air drying but direct exposure to the sun may impair their natural color. After washing, cones may be dried on the radiator or furnace top or they may be spread in a single layer in an open box. Give each cone ample space for expansion since the scales contract when wet and expand as they dry. Some kinds like those of White or Sugar Pine, actually double in size. A popping and cracking noise usually accompanies the opening of the scales. One summer, while motoring home from a vacation, we were certain bandits must be chasing us from the noises of the cones popping open in the trunk of our car!

6. CONES

1. Hemlock   2. Cryptomeria   3. Unopened cones   4. Redwood   5. Knobcone Pine   6. Hemlock   7. Pitch Pine 8. Douglas Fir   9. Pitch Pine   10. Giant Sequoia   11. Pinyon Pine   12. Loblolly Pine   13. Fir   14. White Pine 15. Atlas Cedar   16. Ponderosa   17. White Pine   18. Spruce   19. Ponderosa   20. Jeffrey Pine   21. Sugar Pine 22. Digger Pine.

Pine Cones.   The pines compose an ancient and proud species of trees which grow in widely separated areas of our country.

Sugar Pine, largest of the pines, bears enormous cones which hang in clusters at the very tips of the upper branches. When the scales are open, a cone averages from 10″ to 20″ in length and from 4″ to 6″ in diameter. These large chocolate-brown cones, with a yellow splash on the tip of each scale, are extremely ornamental and prominently used at Christmas.

The White Pine cone is a diminutive edition of those on the Sugar Pine and they too hang in clusters at the tips of the upper branches. The immature cones are cylindrical with the tips of each scale curved tightly inward and look much like a big fat cigar. They are greenish but turn yellow-brown as they mature.

Digger Pine has a large, handsome cone which is one of the heaviest of all the American pine cones. It grows 10″ long and almost as wide. The tip of each reddish-brown scale terminates in a stout triangular hook which protrudes downward and is extremely sharp. Between the scales are oily seeds as large as Lima beans. The Digger Indians harvested large quantities of these seeds, which accounts for the tree's name.

Pinyon Pine is commonly called the Nut Pine because of the quality and quantity of its edible seed kernel. The short, flaring, oblong cone has a vigorous yet artistic character. In some, the tan scales appear to have been sprayed with green and in others with yellow.

The Knobcone Pine has outstanding characteristics. The cones remain on the tree almost indefinitely and seldom liberate the seed until after the death of the tree. These hardy cones, 3" to 6"- long, grow in clusters on the main trunk. The cones are blunt and stubby with tightly locked scales. Their color is gray and they can be used for years without fear of breakage.

Fir Cones. Fir trees are generally cylindrical in shape with their cones standing upright on the stiff branches. Most fir cones must be gathered before they ripen since at maturity the scales and seed fall away, one by one, leaving a stout core axis on the branches.

White Fir has numerous varieties of cones with silvery, yellow or bluish needles. The cylindrical cones, 3" to 5" long, grow near or at the top of the tree.

Red Fir has a light-tan cone 5" long and about half as wide.

Balsam Fir, known as the American Christmas tree, has a cone about 4" long with a violet tone.

Douglas Fir cones are significantly different from those of other firs in possessing a 3-lobed bract on the tips of the scales. These extend beyond the ends of the scales at odd intervals and are a sure way to distinguish the cone. They may be gathered at any time since they do not fall apart at maturity, as do other firs. They are excellent for ornamental uses because of their attractive reddish-brown color and convenient size, 2" to 4".

Spruce Cones. The drooping cones are a distinguishing feature of the spruces.

Norway Spruce is a tall tree often cultivated as an ornamental. The long slender cones, the largest of the spruces, grow to 7".

Colorado Spruce has blue or silver-blue needles. The light-tan cone is 2″ to 4″ long and the scales are thin and flexible.

White Spruce has a small red-brown cone about 1½″ long.

Cedar Cones.　Cedars are among the most beautiful of ornamental trees.

Deodar Cedar has graceful pendulous branches. The warm-brown cones grow upright and are 3″ to 5″ long. The formation resembles a thick, many-petaled flower with the scales tightly clustered about a raised center.

Atlas Cedar is a beautiful tree with feathery bluish-green foliage. Its cones stand erect on the branches and are about 3″ long with a thick symetrical form.

Sequoia Cones.　The Sequoia, though a giant among trees, has very small cones. They mature at the end of their second season and after the scales open to shed the seeds, the cones may be seen hanging on the tree for many years. These cones are scarce since the trees do not produce many and they are the only means of perpetuating the species.

Giant Sequoia cones are about the size and shape of a hen's egg. The scales are thick and when open form a regular criss-cross pattern over the entire cone.

Redwood cones are similar in shape but smaller in size, about 1″ long. The oval brown cones hang down among the feathery branches.

Chart 2. VARIATIONS IN THE SIZE OF SOME CONES

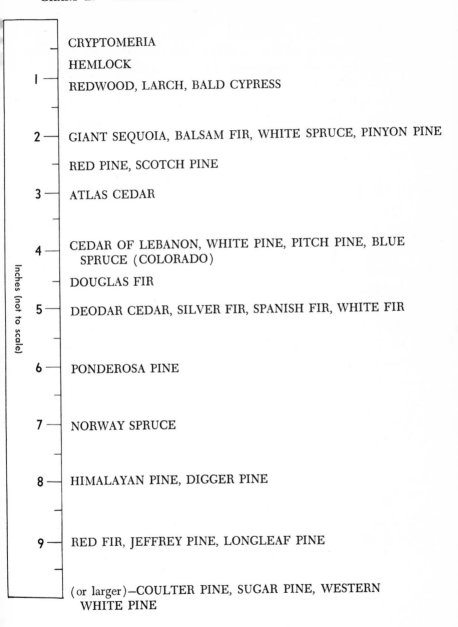

CRYPTOMERIA

HEMLOCK

1 — REDWOOD, LARCH, BALD CYPRESS

2 — GIANT SEQUOIA, BALSAM FIR, WHITE SPRUCE, PINYON PINE

RED PINE, SCOTCH PINE

3 — ATLAS CEDAR

4 — CEDAR OF LEBANON, WHITE PINE, PITCH PINE, BLUE SPRUCE (COLORADO)

DOUGLAS FIR

5 — DEODAR CEDAR, SILVER FIR, SPANISH FIR, WHITE FIR

6 — PONDEROSA PINE

7 — NORWAY SPRUCE

8 — HIMALAYAN PINE, DIGGER PINE

9 — RED FIR, JEFFREY PINE, LONGLEAF PINE

(or larger)—COULTER PINE, SUGAR PINE, WESTERN WHITE PINE

Inches (not to scale)

NUTS

Nuts are the dry fruit of certain trees provided with a hard or woody shell to protect the seed. Nuts, as commonly understood, are the edible varieties, such as Almond, Brazil, Pecan or Walnut, but some of the other kinds develop attractive capsules, hulls or husks. The variety in shape, color and texture of the exterior of a nut is important for ornamental uses. Our country is blessed with many nut trees and fall is the ideal time to gather them. In most areas, if you are a jump ahead of the squirrels, you will find a plentiful supply from which to choose.

Drying of Nuts.   Nuts are easily dried because Nature intended them to last. Wash the nuts in soap and water to remove any dirt on the shell and lay them on a flat surface where there is a circulation of air until dry. Few require more than exposure to the air for several weeks to keep satisfactorily. Add a handful of moth flakes to the container in which the nuts are stored to discourage worms and insects.

DECORATIVE NUTS

Black Walnut is a well-known tree in the eastern part of the United States. The nut is enclosed by a hard shell plus a hull. If they are gathered while the hull is yellow-green and spread in a single layer on a warm surface, in 2 to 3 months they turn into hard, firm, black balls. Some have kept for over 5 years.

Chestnut (edible) and the more plentiful Horse Chestnut have attractive prickly burrs protecting the nut. They are highly decorative especially if they are dried with the burr half open exposing the nut.

Not all Hickory Nuts are good to eat but are adequate for drying. The Shagbark and the Shellbark types have the largest-sized nuts and assume the best color when dried. Often during drying the shell will crack, forming an interesting pattern.

The Acorn of the Oak is a familiar sight nestling on the ground under a tree. Each kind of oak has a different acorn. Some are long and thin, others short and fat and still others have cups covered with moss. If acorns are gathered early in the season, before they start to sprout, they will dry easily and retain a better. color. When an acorn refuses to stay in the cup, use a little glue, replace the acorn with firm pressure, allow to dry, and it will stay for years.

CHART 3. A SELECTION OF PODS FROM TREES, SHRUBS, VINES, ETC.

This selection of seed pods covers only a limited number of the vast quantity available. Technically a pod is a dried fruit that splits open to emit its seeds, like a bean pod, but in general usage pod and seed pod are used interchangeably. Some pods listed may be found in your own area and others may have to be obtained through a commercial source for dried plants.

NAME	GROWS AS	SHAPE	DRIED COLOR
ACACIA	tree or shrub	pea-shaped	green
AGAVE	plant	cluster of oval cups	tan
ALDER, BLACK, *Alnus vulgaris*	tree	cluster	brown
BOTTLE BRUSH, *Callistemon*	tree	small cylinders	gray
BUTTERFLY WEED, *Asclepias tuberosa*	herb	small, long, thin	tan
CASTOR BEAN (Palma Christi), *Ricinus communis*	annual	cluster of burrs	brown
CATALPA (Indian Bean), *Bignonioides*	tree	very long	brown
CATTAIL (Reed), *Typha*	perennial herb	spike	brown

Plant	Type	Shape	Color
CHINESE LANTERN PLANT (Winter Cherry), *Physalis alkekengi*	perennial	ribbed balls	orange
COLUMBINE, *Aquilegia*	perennial	oval, flower-like	tan
DELPHINIUM, garden hybrids	annual herbs	spike	tan
DOCK (Sorrel), *Rumex*	perennial weed	stem of small capsules	tan, brown, green
EUCALYPTUS (Gum Tree)	tree	cluster of bells	tan
FALSE OR WILD INDIGO, *Baptisia*	perennial	spike of ovals	black
GAS PLANT, *Dictamnus albus*	perennial	flower-shaped	tan
GLOBE THISTLE, *Echinops*	herb	prickly balls	blue
HONESTY (Moonwort or Satinflower), *Lunaria annua*	perennial	oval disk	white
IRIS, SIBERIAN, *Iris sibirica*	perennial	oval	tan
JACARANDA	tree	shell-shaped	gray
LILAC, *Syringa*, single or hybrid	shrub	small clusters	brown
LOCUST, *Robinia*	tree	twisted, long	brown
LOTUS, *Nelumbium*	aquatic	flattened cone	brown
MAGNOLIA (Bull Bay), *Magnolia grandiflora*	tree	large oval cluster	brown
MILKWEED (Silkweed), *Asclepias*	herb	boat-shaped	green, tan
MIMOSA	shrub or tree	pea-shaped	green

A SELECTION OF PODS FROM TREES, SHRUBS, VINES, ETC. (*Cont.*)

Name	Grows as	Shape	Dried Color
MOTH MULLEIN, *Verbascum blattaria*	herb	spike of small buttons	brown
MULLEIN (Candlewick), *Verbascum thapsus*	herb	spike of small cups	tan
OKRA (Gumbo), *Hibiscus esculentus*	plant	long, ridged, oval	tan
PAULOWNIA	tree	oval capsule	brown
PEONY, *Paeonia*, single or double varieties	perennial	flower forms	brown
PLANTAIN LILY (Funkia), *Hosta*	perennial herb	spike of elongated capsules	green
POINCIANA, ROYAL, *Delonix regia*	tree	woody, very long	brown
POPPY, ORIENTAL, *Papaver orientale*	perennial	cup-shaped	tan
ROSE OF SHARON (Shrub Althea), *Hibiscus syriacus*	shrub	clustered capsules	tan, brown
SENNA, *Cassia*	shrub	thin, long	brown
SILK TREE, *Albizzia julibrissin*	tree	long	green
SNEEZEWEED, *Helenium*	herb	flat capsules	black

Name	Type	Form	Color
STERCULIA	tree	cluster	cocoa, yellow seed
SWEET GUM, *Liquidambar*	tree	spiked capsule	dark tan
SWEET PEA, PERENNIAL, *Lathyrus latifolius*	vine	long	tan, green
SYCAMORE (Buttonwood), *Platanus occidentalis*	tree	soft, round, thin	tan
TEASEL, *Dipsacus*	biennial herb	spiky heads	green, tan, black
TORNILLO (Screw Bean), *Strombocarpa odorata*	shrub	tightly coiled	tan
TRAVELER'S-TREE, *Ravenala madagascariensis*	tree	woody capsule cluster	brown, blue seed
TREE OF HEAVEN, *Ailanthus altissima*	tree	dense clusters	green
TRUMPET VINE, *Campsis radicans*	vine	long	brown
TULIP, *Tulipa*, Cottage or Darwin	bulb	oval	tan
WILD BERGAMOT, *Monarda fistulosa*	herb	tiny pincushions	brown
WISTERIA	vine	long, velvety	green
WOMAN'S-TONGUE TREE, *Albizzia lebbek*	tree	long, thin	brown
WOOD ROSES (Ceylon Morning-glory), *Ipomoea tuberosa*	vine	groups flower forms	tan, brown
YUCCA, *Yucca filamentosa*	plant	cluster	tan

6. Flowers for Arrangements

There are many ways to dry flowers but no matter which method you choose, the problem of removal of moisture from the flower is the same. This chapter is devoted to a discussion of methods for the drying of flowers in an agent but in some instances the hanging method is suggested as an alternate one. The details of hanging were discussed in Chapter 4.

Flowers which are processed in an agent retain a more natural form and a greater degree of color, than by any other method. The secret of success in keeping natural color and dimensional form is speed in removal of moisture. By covering a flower in an absorbent substance (an agent), you not only speed withdrawal of moisture but set the color by preventing exposure to light during drying. Once you are cognizant of certain facts and have tried a few flowers in an agent you will discover how comparatively easy it is to dry lots of flowers. It will always be a thrilling experience to have a natural, colorful flower come out of the agent.

The discovery of an old book in our family collection started my experiments in the drying of flowers. Over a number of years this book has been the inspiration for my experiments and many of the principles are still the basis of some of my drying methods. The quaint, intricate recipes in stilted Victorian language are interesting to read but times have changed since 1864 and the methods need improvement to meet our present standards.

AGENTS AND METHODS

A variety of substances can be used as agents for drying flowers. Some of those I have tested are cornstarch, powdered sugar, fuller's earth, alum, powdered pumice, salt, borax, sand and corn meal. There is a real advantage in using commercial items since they do not need to be prepared prior to use. Borax has been widely publicized as an agent. It is effective and one of its favorable points is the time element, since no more than a week is required to dry most flowers. Trial will show you how many kinds of flowers can be dried satisfactorily in this agent.

When you are enthusiastic about drying flowers you are continually in search of a foolproof medium for all types. In handling agents and noting their effects on flowers, certain facts become evident. Often there will be a period of rain or extreme dampness when the garden abounds in bloom. If you cut flowers at a time when there is a particle of moisture on the petals, a soft fine powder, such as borax, powdered pumice or sugar will lump or cling to the flower after it is dry. Also a soft powder substance cakes and cracks leaving portions of the flower exposed. Therefore I found it necessary to add something to roughen and coarsen the mixture. A grain cereal, like Wheatena, Cream of Wheat or corn meal, does the trick. I have become convinced that a combination of substances, when used as an agent, far surpasses a single element for drying a majority of flowers. Adding uniodized salt has kept color brighter in the flowers.

Of the many possible combinations, my favorites are simple and easy. You will have success with either of the following combinations:

Equal proportions of powdered pumice and yellow corn meal *or* equal proportions of borax and yellow corn meal.

To each quart of either of the above mixtures, add 3 tablespoons of salt.

These items are inexpensive and easy to obtain. It is not necessary to purchase a large quantity of any one because several boxes are all the average person will need during a season.

The two most important points to watch for in drying any flowers successfully are: to process the flower before it has passed its color prime, and not to allow flowers to remain in the agent longer than necessary. The following descriptions of agent methods are the result of trial and test with many types and kinds of flowers and, if directions are followed, the methods will be successful for you. Once you become careless in handling details, failures will follow.

Combined-Agent Method #1

CHOICE AND PREPARATION OF RECEPTACLE

Choose a receptacle that is large enough to hold the flowers without crowding. This can be made of pasteboard, plastic, wood or metal. Line the receptacle with waxed or florist paper.

Pour the agent into the receptacle until it reaches a depth of ½″ and covers the bottom evenly.

FLOWERS—CUTTING AND PREPARATION

Cut the flowers on a sunny day, at the time you feel they have the least amount of moisture on the petals. In general, flowers which are not fully developed retain the best color. Flowers should be fresh and crisp, never droopy.

To lessen the moisture content, strip all of the foliage from the stem, except possibly 1 or 2 leaves near the head.

An average length for the stem of a round or ball-shaped flower is 6″ to 8″. Stalk-type flowers, such as Delphinium, Gladiolus or Stock, may be 12″ to 18″. Foliage may be kept and dried too.

POSITION OF THE FLOWERS

Place the flowers to be dried on the agent in the receptacle in any one of various positions. Flowers with large heads like Dahlias, Marigolds, Mums or Zinnias are processed face down and stem up. Stalk-type flowers like Delphinium or Gladiolus are placed in the receptacle in a horizontal position or head down in a tubular receptacle. A flower like the Tulip can be opened and the petals spread wide. Parrot Tulips respond wonderfully to this treatment.

HANDLING THE AGENT

After the flower is placed satisfactorily, add small quantities of the agent to the flower with a tablespoon. Work it in between and around the petals to keep the form natural. Keep adding small amounts of the agent until the flower is covered and actually buried in it. Use only a quantity sufficient to cover the flower because the weight of more than just enough may alter its form or shape. The stem of the flower is left uncovered and protruding above the agent. Flowers are dried in a single layer in the receptacle. One layer should never be be dried upon another. The *receptacle is left open* during the entire drying time.

TIME OF DRYING

Chart 4, page 100, suggests periods of time required for drying various kinds of flowers. If you want to try other flowers than those mentioned, just remember the general principle that large or thick flowers hold greater amounts of moisture and therefore will require more time than small or thin ones. At the end of the suggested drying time, test the flowers by inserting a finger in the agent and feeling if the flower petals have stiffened or if they should remain longer to become dry.

REMOVAL OF FLOWERS

When the flowers are dry, gently ease the agent away from the petals with your fingers and carefully lift the flower out of the receptacle. If the stem is gently tapped against the side of the receptacle it will usually dislodge any remaining agent but if some particles persist in clinging to the petals, they may be whisked away with a small soft camel's-hair brush such as an artist uses. It may be necessary to moisten the brush slightly in order to remove stubborn bits. An excess of water will impair the color you have preserved—use it sparingly.

I have found that moistening a soft brush with vegetable oil and brushing the petals of velvet-textured flowers like Pansies and Snapdragons will restore their texture, sometimes lost during drying. This should be done carefully with a light touch.

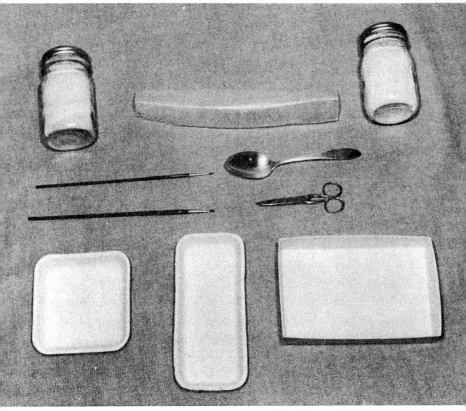

Robert Scharff

7. USING AN AGENT

Here is all the equipment needed for drying flowers in an agent: two jars of a combined agent, waxed paper to line boxes, brushes to clean the dried flowers, a spoon to handle the agent, scissors to clip with and, at the bottom, boxes of different sizes to hold the flowers.

Such flowers will appear glossy when first done but after a week in the air will resume their natural velvety texture.

STORAGE OF FLOWERS AND AGENT

Once the flowers are dried they are ready for use at a future date if stored in a covered box. Flowers should never be left in the agent indefinitely. The agent does not deteriorate if kept in a sealed container.

Combined-Agent Method #2. Recently while admiring a shipment of Gardenias at the florist, I thought the manner in which they were packed would be an excellent way to place flowers for drying. After considerable experimentation I have found the following procedure results in good color and natural form for the majority of round, many-petaled flowers. It is particularly adaptable to Daffodils, Marigolds, Peonies, Roses, Tulips and Zinnias. In time this heads-up placement may supersede the inverted position for my drying.

CHOICE AND PREPARATION OF BOX

Select a sturdy pasteboard box from 12" to 18" long, 6" to 8" wide, and 2" deep.

Line it with waxed paper and at intervals punch small holes in the bottom. The holes should be big enough for the stems to go through easily but not so large that the agent can sift out. Space the holes so that there will be at least 1" of agent between each flower.

Support the box at each corner, 8" above the drying table or shelf, thus avoiding tipping or spilling.

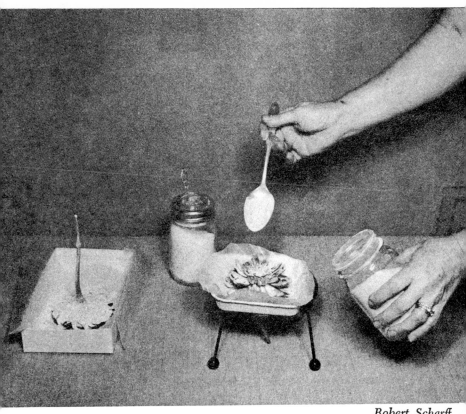

8. USING AN AGENT

This shows two flowers being dried by the combined-agent method. On the left a flower has been partially covered in a heads-down position and on the right another one is being covered in a heads-up position.

FLOWERS—CUTTING AND PREPARATION

Select, cut and prepare flowers as previously described in Method #1, using 6" stems.

Snip thorns from rose stems and bulky parts of other stems.

POSITION OF FLOWERS

Insert a stem in each hole and pull it through until the under side of the flower rests on the bottom of the box and its stem protrudes below.

HANDLING THE AGENT

Work the combined agent under the flower, between the petals and around each flower, ultimately covering the entire flower. Once in position do not move or cover the box during the drying.

TIME OF DRYING

Consult Chart 4, page 100, for suggested time of drying.

REMOVAL OF FLOWERS

After the flowers are dry, tilt the box and allow the agent to run out slowly over the edge of the box. Pour out as much as you possibly can and then leave the flowers in position for 24 hours. During this time they will absorb enough moisture from the air to be easy to handle. Remove gently by pushing on the stem to loosen flower and proceed to remove agent as described in Method #1.

Other Agents. If you prefer a single substance, like borax, powdered pumice or fuller's earth, you can use it to replace the combined agent and process in the same way. However, if you plan to use salt or sand, the variations in the process are noted below.

Salt is an excellent agent to dry certain flowers like Delphinium and Larkspur. It will produce the best results if kept moderately warm during the entire drying time. Heat in excess of 100° F. alters the color of the flowers.

Sand is one of the oldest known agents for use on flowers and is supposed to have originated in Germany. You will need a lot of fine sand prepared by washing and pouring off the water until all soluble particles are gone. The sand must be completely dry before use. Pass the sand through a medium-sized mesh sieve so that all foreign matter is removed. Beach sand is appropriate since washing removes any excess of salt and sieving removes any particles that might harm the petals of a flower. Marigolds, Zinnias, Roses and other garden flowers can be dried in sand.

METHOD FOR USING SAND

Cut flowers in fully developed state. The height of the box will determine the length of the stem. Take care that there is no moisture or dew on the petals. Pour 1" or 2" of water in a glass and place 3 or 4 of the flower stems in it for about an hour, thus allowing them to suck in enough water to prevent wilting during the first stage of drying.

Choose a strong box (pasteboard or wood) which is large enough to hold the flowers. Line it with heavy paper and pour 1" of sand on the bottom. Place flowers vertically on the sand in the box, either head down and stem up or stem down and head up, but in either case the stem should be short enough to allow ½" of sand below the box cover.

The next job calls for deft handling since flower and stem must be entirely covered with the sand. Using a funnel or spoon slowly pour the sand until every particle of the flower rests in it. Then you place the box in a warm dry place, taking care not to shake it. Too low a temperature will rot the flowers and too high will scorch their color. Place the cover on the box and forget it for 3 or 4 weeks.

When you are sure the flowers are fully dried, open the box and, holding it on a slant, let the sand run out. Lift each flower out by the stem, turn it upside down and if necessary shake gently to remove grains of sand. Flowers are brittle in such a dry state and require care in handling. After a few days' exposure to the air the flowers are much less brittle. Keep the sand in a sealed container to be used again.

Everyone may not be a dried-flower enthusiast but a few trials in one of the methods described will make you eager to become one. Any person with imagination can visualize the vast possibilities of colorful dried flowers to cheer and beautify the home during the bleak days of winter. Spring and summer are rich in bloom and it costs little in time and money to keep some of this beauty.

FLOWERS ANYONE CAN DRY

Acacia, often called Mimosa by the florist, will keep its bright yellow color for months when dried. The soft fuzzy appearance is lost while drying but the miniature yellow balls remain on the stem. The finely cut silvery-gray foliage may be left on the stem to form a pleasing contrast. Hang in bunches of not more than 3 until the stem is brittle.

The *China Aster* today has fascinating forms and many of the double varieties are suited to drying. The 2″ to 3″ flowers in lavender, purple, pink and crimson retain color when they are dried in the combined agent.

Bells of Ireland is an odd and interesting plant which has become very popular in recent years. The tall erect stems are closely covered with small yet perfect bell-shaped forms called bracts. Their color is a lovely soft green and as they are paper thin, they appear to be translucent. In the center of each of these bells is a small flower and as the plant matures the flower drops out, leaving the stem of green bells. For drying, it is best to cut the stalk before all of the flowers fall, because at a later stage the color may turn neutral. Bells of Ireland may be dried either by hanging or in the combined agent.

Celosia is a fascinating plant which has been a popular garden annual since the eighteenth century. The harsh ugly colors have been greatly refined by hybridization. Celosia has two easily distinguishable forms: the tall feathery spike of *Celosia plumosa* and the stiff fluted crests of *Celosia cristata*. The common name of Cockscomb is well suited to the stiff fluted crests which bear a decided resemblance to a rooster's comb. The feathery spikes of Celosia are handsome in the garden but the crests are better for drying.

In drying Celosia, two things must be remembered: First, the heads should be gathered before they are fully mature or the seeds will begin to drop. Second, they should not be picked after a hard rain or during a damp spell. All the foliage is stripped from each stem and I recommend removing as much as possible of the fuzz on the broader upper part of the stem without harming the sturdy crest. Each stem is hung individually upside down as described in Chapter 4. This has proved to be the best way

9. GARDEN FLOWERS

1. Roses   2. Cosmos   3. Cosmos   4. Zinnias   5. Snapdragons   6. Delphinium   7. Marigolds.

to dry this type of flower. Celosia needs to dry slowly—it may take 3 weeks or more—and the process should not be hastened by artificial heat. Often a head will appear limp and absolutely worthless immediately before it is dry. Yellow, orange and green are fascinating in color when fresh but they lose much of their color when dry. Pink, rose and red will retain color for several years.

Delphinium is one of the easiest flowers to dry. Despite the fact that it is considered fragile, the paper-thin petals in the small florets dry quickly and hold color. They may become a tone lighter or darker but the color always remains clear and pleasing. Delphiniums may be dried in salt or the combined agent. Larkspur, with the same family characteristics, will also dry excellently.

In the *Everlasting* family there is a wide choice for drying. The paperlike quality of these flowers is especially suitable. Everlastings are comparatively easy to grow and you will be surprised at how many flowers a dozen plants will produce. Strawflowers are the best known and the largest of the Everlastings. The newer varieties come in many colors including white. If you harvest this type of flower when ⅓ to ½ open you will find it fully opened when dry. The stem is stripped and the flowers bunched and hung as described in Chapter 4. Flowers may be dried on their own stem or the stem replaced by inserting a wire into the flower head. All Strawflowers purchased at the florist are dried on wire stems. The yellow and orange heads are perfect for fall, while rose, lavender or pink flowers can be used at any time of year. Statice is known by a number of common names such as Thrift, Sea Pink or Sea Lavender. Statice is as colorful as the rainbow with shades of lavender, pink, rose, blue, yellow and creamy white. The long arched stems are so graceful and pleasing that they are adaptable to many uses. Statice might be called a foolproof material for drying because no matter how you treat it, it will dry well. Several sprays, forgotten by accident, dried perfectly with no treatment. However, to be sure of usable material, cut when the small flowers are not fully open, bind into loose bunches and hang with the flower heads downward. If you buy Statice and it droops by the time you reach home, recut the stems and place them in warm water until the flowers become stiff again. Wipe the stems free of moisture and hang in bunches. Globe Amaranth, with its papery, clover-shaped heads, is grown for its lasting quality. The flowers, rose, purple, yellow or white, are cut for drying only when fully matured. Bunch 5 or 6 stems and hang.

Baby's-Breath is an old stand-by in borders or rock gardens. The annual variety grows in pink or white. Baby's-Breath may be dried satisfactorily if picked when the flowers are partially open and hung. This plant material is excellent as a filler to soften or add a light touch to mass- or period-arrangement designs.

Heath and *Heather* are often used interchangeably to denote the members of the Heath family. Heather, though originally a native of Europe, seems to be well adapted to our country. The long and beautifully colored spikes of the lavender and pink varieties are easy to dry. They should be processed when the young blooms are bright in color and are hung to dry. The variety which the florist calls "Regina" is one of the best. White sprays have a tendency to become dull and gray.

Hydrangea with its large clusters of showy florets has a wide range of color. The Oriental name "flower of a thousand moods" is highly appropriate. Hydrangeas dry well and success depends on harvesting. The blue, pink and lavender ones of the Asiatic variety should be gathered when the small florets are crisp, fresh and colorful and dried in the combined agent. The green or white flowers of the treelike plants undergo tissue changes later in their growth when tresses become papery and the color deepens. This is the time to gather lovely shades of deep green and white tinged with rose or wine color. Dry these Hydrangeas by hanging in small bunches.

Lilacs have undergone many horticultural changes and now their florets are of many colors and sizes. The larger the floret, the better it will dry. The French hybrids, with pink, purple or white heads, dry excellently. Lilacs should be cut before they are in full bloom if they are to retain color and there should be as little moisture as possible on the florets. Lilacs need ample room in the drying box because if they are crowded or placed upon one another, the shape will be distorted when they are dry.

Marigolds are popular flowers to supply color in the garden and they are divided into two main classifications. Those varieties which have small flowers are called French, while those with large flowers are termed African. The larger ones are the best for drying since Marigolds shrink when they are dry. The ball shapes of the double varieties offer many opportunities. A range of color can be obtained

10. GARDEN FLOWERS

1. Acacia   2. Narcissuses   3. Parrot Tulip   4. Lilac   5.
Pansies   6. Parrot Tulip   7. Tulip   8. Peonies.

by drying some in yellow and others in orange. Guinea Gold, one of the oldest of the improved varieties, has always dried well. Like many other flowers, Marigolds are picked before fully developed. If the agent is worked in between the petals and around the head of a Marigold it will keep its ball shape. Marigolds take longer than some other flowers to dry because of the thickness of the flower. The heads-up method is recommended for them.

The *Peony* is called by the Chinese the "King of Flowers" and there are not many others which can compare with it for sheer beauty. The showy flower heads and luxurious growth of the ball types have been popular garden perennials for many years. The flower dries very well but requires a deep box in which to hold the large flower shape. I have found that they dry better if each one is processed separately in its own box. The Single and Japanese Peonies are among the most satisfactory of all flowers to dry. If they are placed face down on the agent and the petals spread wide open, when dry they will resemble crepe-paper flowers. The center retains its color and petals, red, pink or white, hold color.

Roses are probably the best-loved of all flowers and among the loveliest of all dried plants. The majority of roses can be dried, with the exception of the Cabbage or Single types. For best results, roses should be picked when ⅔ to ¾ open, since they continue to open during drying. A full-blown rose will fall apart easily after drying. Roses may be dried in sand or the combined agent. The heads-up method has been especially successful with Hybrid Tea and Floribundas. The latter have sterling qualities for dry-

11. DRIED ROSES

Coral Dawn climbing roses with their own foliage form a design that gives year-round enjoyment reminiscent of summer beauty.

ing and any of the popular ones, such as Pinocchio, Fashion or Goldilocks, retain good color. Many of the larger-flowered climbing roses, such as the Dawns or Paul Scarlet, can be dried. (Illustration 11.) For drying, yellow, pink or red roses hold color, though some reds dry almost black. Some roses retain a slight fragrance.

Wandflower has long wandlike spikes up to 2′ in length. These spikes are covered with small, long florets of reddish-purple or salmon-pink, each with a yellow throat. They dry beautifully if hung in bunches of not more than 3 stems. Your florist may refer to this plant as a French Heather.

Zinnias are fine flowers for drying and the hybridizer has provided us with many colors. The stiff stem and erect heads of the large-flower varieties, like Cactus, Dahlia and Giant, are better than those of the smaller Lilliput types. Zinnias wilt quickly so they should be processed immediately after cutting. If this is impossible, their stems should be placed in water to revive them before they are processed. Zinnias of all colors dry well. Red and lavender become deeper, while pink, yellow and orange remain about the same. Unlike Marigolds, Zinnias do not change perceptibly in size.

Chart 4. TIMING FOR DRYING FLOWERS IN COMBINED AGENT

This chart lists some of the better-known flowers which have been dried successfully. It can be used as a guide for drying the flowers mentioned and for selecting others with the same physical characteristics of size, thickness and texture.

Name	Processed	Days Drying	Colors to Dry
ASTER, CHINA, *Callistephus chinensis*	singly	5– 7	lavender, pink
BABY GLADIOLUS, *Gladiolus tristis*	spike	6– 8	white
BLACK-EYED SUSAN, *Rudbeckia hirta*	singly	8–10	yellow
BUTTERFLY BUSH, *Buddleia*	spike	5– 7	purple, pink
BUTTERFLY WEED, *Asclepias tuberosa*	head	5– 7	orange
CANTERBURY BELLS, *Campanula medium*	stalk	7–10	blue, lavender, pink
CHRYSANTHEMUM, pompon, single or Korean annual varieties	spray	6– 7–8	yellow, red, pink
COLUMBINE, *Aquilegia*, long- or short-spurred	spray	4– 6	deep colors
CORNFLOWER (Bachelor's-Button), *Centaurea cyanus*	singly	4– 6	pink, blue
COSMOS, *Cosmos bipinnatus*	singly	4– 6	white, pink, crimson

Name			
DAFFODIL, *Narcissus pseudo-narcissus,* large trumpet Narcissus	singly	4– 5	yellow
DAHLIA, pompon, single, collarette	singly	6– 8	yellow, red, pink
DAISY, PAINTED (Pyrethrum), *Chrysanthemum coccineum*	singly	4– 6	crimson, lavender
DAISY, OXEYE, *Chrysanthemum leucanthemum*	singly	4– 6	white
DAY LILY, *Hemerocallis*	singly	6– 8	all colors
DELPHINIUM, hybrid variety	stalk	4– 6	blue, violet
GLADIOLUS	stalk	7–10	most colors
GLOXINIA, *Sinningia speciosa*	singly	8–10	solid colors
GOLDENROD, *Solidago*	stalk	4– 6	yellow
HYDRANGEA, Asiatic variety	singly	7–10	blue, pink, purple
LARKSPUR, *Delphinium ajacis,* annual variety	stalk	4– 6	blue, pink, lavender
LIATRIS (Blazing Star) or (Button Snakeroot)	spike	8–10	purple
LILAC, *Syringa,* common or double-flowered variety	heads	8–10	all colors
LILY, *Lilium auratum* or *L. umbellatum* types	singly	8–10	all colors
LILY OF THE VALLEY, *Convallaria majalis*	singly	4– 6	white, pink
MARIGOLD, AFRICAN, *Tagetes erecta*	singly	8–10	all colors
NARCISSUS, *Narcissus barri,* short-cupped Daffodil	singly	4– 5	yellow

TIMING FOR DRYING FLOWERS IN COMBINED AGENT (*Cont.*)

NAME	PROCESSED	DAYS DRYING	COLORS TO DRY
PANSY (Heartsease), *Viola tricolor hortensis*	singly	4– 6	deep colors
PEONY, *Paeonia*, single, Japanese, semidouble	singly	6– 8	pink, red
QUEEN ANNE'S LACE (Wild Carrot), *Daucus carota*	singly	4– 5	white
ROSE, polyantha, floribunda, hybrid tea	singly	8–10	yellow, pink, red
SNAPDRAGON (Toad's-Mouth), *Antirrhinum majus*	stem	6– 8	lavender, yellow, pink, red
STOCK (Brampton), *Mathiola incana*	stalk	8–10	lavender, purple, pink
SWEET PEA, PERENNIAL, *Lathyrus lattfolius*	stem	4– 6	deep values
SWEET PEA, *Lathyrus odoratus*	stem	4– 6	deep values
TRITOMA (Poker Plant), *Kniphofia*	singly	8–10	orange
TULIP, *Tulipa*, cottage, Darwin or parrot	singly	6– 8	all colors
ZINNIA, giant, Dahlia or cactus	singly	6– 8	all colors

7. Foliage for Arrangements

Leaves are such a common sight that we take them for granted. But each leaf is a complex food-manufacturing organism for the plant without which it could not exist. Leaves vary enormously in their size, form, color, marking and veining and this diversity in physical character adds to their ornamental value. The difference between an ordinary or outstanding dried arrangement lies in the effective use of foliage. Often such leaves as Canna, Sea Grape or Cecropia furnish a finishing touch otherwise lacking in a dried design.

Technically, the term foliage denotes only green leaves but in general usage it is applied collectively to the leaves of all plants no matter what their color. Leaves, with their natural function of transpiration, are admirably suited to drying since this process continues during treatment of a leaf. Though easily dried, some leaves do require special handling to retain maximum color and natural form. In general, the best time to gather leaves for drying is in the earliest part of their growing season when their color is fresh and clear. The later the leaf is cut, the greater will be the loss of color when it is dry. For example, the leaves of the Beech, gathered in spring, will remain green but if cut in fall they will turn tan and after a hard freeze may actually become white when they are dry.

The method by which foliage is dried determines its finished form. A large single leaf dried in a flat form serves one purpose while the same leaf dried with a curve gives an entirely different result. Small leaves are usually more effective when they are dried on the branch. Naturally, the dried shape of a leaf will be determined by the type of foliage and the design in which it is to be used.

SIX METHODS FOR DRYING FOLIAGES

(1) *Pressing.* This method produces leaves which are flat in form and it is suitable for either a single leaf like Ivy, or leaves on a stem or branch like Shallon. Place a single layer of leaf material between several thicknesses of an absorbent paper. Newspapers will do. Adjust the shape of each leaf as you place it on the paper, by either curving or straightening it, since little change can be made in a leaf after it is dried. If you want to be certain that the color in the leaf holds true, replace the papers with fresh ones after 24 hours. Any quantity of foliage, either large or small, can be processed at the same time as one layer is piled upon another with thicknesses of paper between each layer. Place an evenly distributed weight on top of the pile to supply the necessary pressure. Leaves will dry in about

a month but they may safely remain in the paper up to 6 months without loss of color.

(2) *Hanging.* Hanging upside down produces leaves which have form and depth. This method is good for large leaves like Canna, a rosette of leaves like Silverleaf, or a branch of leaves like Horse Chestnut. Hang as described in Chapter 4.

(3) *Evaporation.* This is an easy way to obtain graceful and often exotically shaped dried leaves. Place the foliage on an absorbent paper in a dry spot for about 2-3 weeks while the moisture evaporates. Do not cover the leaves but turn them over once or twice to promote even drying. Leaves to process in this way are Canna, Orchid, Rubber Plant, Sea Grape, Magnolia, Lotus, Castor Bean and Aspidistra.

(4) *Watering.* This somewhat specialized method is not adaptable to all foliages. Leaves to be dried by this method should be large, strong in texture, and have a considerable length of stem. Cut the stem of the leaf on a 45° angle and place in a container (a tall one is best), in which there is about 2″ of water. In about a week, the water will evaporate and the leaf begin to turn color. Add no more water but let the leaf remain in the container until it is completely dry to the touch. The weight of the leaf may curve the stem but this can be adjusted during drying. Leaves to dry in this way are Calla, Castor Bean, Dracaena, Galax, Lotus and Shallon.

(5) *Glycerinizing.* Leaves which are treated with a glycerine solution will last indefinitely. The classification of this foliage as a dried plant is a broad interpretation of the term. They are neither stiff nor unpliable like other dried plants but they are as long lasting and certainly they are not fresh.

There are no hard and fast rules as to which foliages can be preserved in glycerine but always use leaves or branches which absorb water freely and are entirely fresh and perky.

Make a solution composed of ⅓ glycerine to ⅔ water and fill a container with it to a depth of 4″ to 5″. To assure complete absorption of the solution, slash the stem of the leaf or branch with a knife or mash it with a hammer for about 1″ at the cut end. Place the stem or branch in the solution and allow it to remain until saturated. This condition is easy to determine since the color of the leaves will change and the edges will begin to ooze. Some leaves reach saturation in a few days while others require several weeks. While in the solution, the foliage should be allowed a free circulation of air and never be covered.

Glycerine changes the color of leaves and the reaction will vary according to the type of foliage and the time of year it is processed. If leaves are picked in spring they are likely to turn red, while if gathered in the fall they usually turn brown. I have found that foliage absorbs the solution more readily during the warmer months. Many of the smaller and thinner types of leaves, like Beech or Red Maple, must be watched for signs of drooping or wilting. If this occurs, they should be removed from the solution and hung upside down for several days. This usually restores their crispness because they have absorbed enough of the solution to be lasting. Large leaves, like Dracaena, may show signs of drying before the solution has had a chance to reach all of the outer edges. If this happens, trim the edges of each leaf neatly with scissors.

Leaves which have been treated in this way may be used in any type of arrangement since placing the stems in water for a short time will do them no harm. Some of those in my collection have been used over a period of 4 years without deterioration. Other possible leaves for processing in this way are mentioned in Chart 5, page 117.

(6) *Skeletonizing.* The process of converting a leaf into a skeleton is not hard but it is a little messy and often smelly. The green or perishable parts of the leaf must be destroyed while the network of veins must be kept intact. Hard or glossy textured leaves, like Holly, Ivy, Magnolia, Maple or Oak, usually process successfully. Only perfect leaves can be used as any imperfections become prominent in the skeleton. Place the leaves in a large receptacle of water and soak them until the green matter comes off easily. (The time needed, 2 to 3 weeks, results in a rather rancid mass of vegetation.) At the end of this time place a few of the leaves in another pan of water and rub each one to expose the veins. Use the thumb and forefinger to remove the green matter, under water. The remaining veins are tender and tear easily so use extreme care in handling. Dry the skeleton between folds of a soft towel before bleaching.

Put the leaf skeleton in a clear, covered jar and bleach

to produce a phantom-shadow look, using 1 tablespoon of bleach to 1 quart of water. Watch the process for whiteness and take care not to let the leaves remain overtime in the bleach or they will become too brittle to handle. Wash the skeletons very carefully in clear water and pour them out on a piece of paper. Before they are quite dry, place them between fresh absorbent paper and press until completely dry.

The skeletonizing method is not recommended because it is much easier to purchase processed leaves from a commercial source. However, their exquisitely fine quality is an excellent foil for the lighter colors and types of dried plant materials in arrangements. Quite appropriately these leaves are called Angel's Wings.

TREE FOLIAGES

Everyone is familiar with the trees in his neighborhood, yet how many people have ever thought that much of this foliage can be dried? A wealth of interesting green leaves can be dried, from the first moment of spring until the leaves begin to color. In the fall Maples and Oaks are famous for their flaming red and orange foliages. Should you

12. FOLIAGES

1. Ivy   2. Spiral Eucalyptus   3. Red Maple   4. Maple
5. Galax   6. Mulberry   7. Lance Eucalyptus   8. Flat Eucalyptus   9. Lemon   10. Beech   11. Tulip Tree   12. Oak
13. Rubber Plant   14. Orchid   15. Sea Grape   16. Croton
17. Magnolia   18. Silver Tree   19. Canna (rolled)   20. Canna (flat).

Vincent Renna

wish to dry these glorious colored leaves, they must be gathered when they first become brilliant. Later in the season the process by which Nature bares her branches for winter has begun and the leaves lose color and fall easily from their stems when dry.

Beech leaves are one of the most accommodating of foliages and all colors, green, copper or purple, dry exceptionally well. The stage at which to cut for various colors was mentioned in the opening paragraphs of this chapter.

The leaves of the Magnolia tree are as attractive as its beautiful flowers. All dry well; Tropical or Grandiflora is one of the best.

Oak leaves process beautifully. The glossy green leaves of spring offer a distinctly different touch to dried designs. For fall color, gather the branches when the leaves begin to change and the veins are still green.

The leaves of Horse Chestnut invariably twist and curl into fascinating shapes when they are hung upside down to dry.

Other tree foliages are mentioned in Chart 5.

GARDEN FOLIAGES

Every home garden has many leaves suitable for drying. Some of the commonly grown plants are mentioned below while others are listed in Chart 5.

Artemisia, Dusty Miller, Cat's-Ear and Wooly Lamb's-Ear retain their soft gray tones and are extremely valuable in arrangements. Cut the Artemisia when it is fully developed, usually in early fall; the others may be picked at any time they are of useful size.

Canna leaves, both green and brown, are exceptional for drying. The best time to pick these leaves is during the midseason of growth. Do not limit the drying of Canna leaves to a flat form but roll some and curl others. When fresh, roll the leaf lengthwise inserting as you roll a single thickness of paper napkin. This helps remove moisture from all surfaces at the same time. After 24 hours, replace the paper with a fresh piece and let it remain in the rolled leaf until it is completely dry. Hang or lay the leaf on a flat surface for about 10 days.

The drying of herbs was discussed in Chapter 4.

Hosta and Day Lily have leaves which become paperlike and transparent. They should be picked in midsummer.

Iris, Gladiolus, Yucca and Peruvian Daffodil, with their long, pointed leaves can be dried for line materials. Iris keeps a better color if picked in early summer but Gladiolus and Yucca can be gathered at any time. Peruvian Daffodils can be cut after they bloom or when the bulbs are lifted from the ground.

Ivy leaves will remain green if they are picked in the fall.

Peony foliage is seldom dried yet it retains color well. If you wish to keep the color green, gather and press the leaves at the time the flowers bloom.

HOUSE-PLANT FOLIAGES

Today most everyone has house plants and the leaves of many dry beautifully. Some plants will be mentioned under tropical foliages which are often grown as house plants and so will not be discussed here.

Philodendron, so easy to grow, is one of the most popular of all house plants. Any of its interesting and varied leaf patterns can be dried but the larger ones are the best.

A great majority of the large and handsome leaves of Dracaena dry well but in some cases the beautiful leaf markings may be lost when they are completely dry. You will find many uses for the long narrow leaves.

Rubber Plant has oblong-shaped leaves almost as indestructible as the plant itself. Many turn a beautiful golden-yellow when they are dry.

Anthurium is generally associated with spectacular bloom but its plain foliage is one of the best for drying. When it is dry, the veining in the leaf stands out and forms interesting patterns.

Leaves from the Begonia or Caladium, with their fragile texture, have not proved practical for drying. Geranium leaves although they hold form will not retain color.

TROPICAL FOLIAGES

Tropical foliages are an outstanding group of leaves with bold, striking forms, unusual coloring and markings. They are tough and durable which is not always true of other dried leaves. Another advantage of tropical leaves is that they may be used fresh first and then dried.

Palms are usually spoken of as the aristocrats of the tropics because of their stately shapes and abundant foliage. Florida, Date, Coconut and Palmetto are the best-known palms. The broad leaves of the fan-type Palm can be cut into varying sizes and are easily molded to a desired line before they are dried.

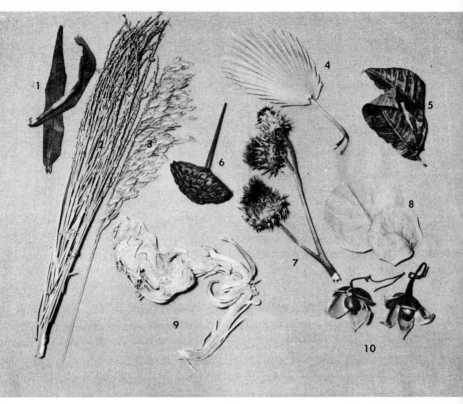

Robert Scharff

13. TROPICAL PLANTS

1. Orchid 2. Date Palm 3. Sea Grape 4. Fan Palm
5. Croton 6. Lotus 7. Cardone 8. Sea Grape 9. Embryo Palm 10. Wood Roses.

Cycas has been used as decorative material for centuries. It grows out-of-doors in warm climates but is also used in the greenhouse or conservatory. The large plume of small green leaves resembling a fern ranges from 8″ to 28″ in length. When fresh, they can be manipulated into graceful lines or curves and dried that way. One or two of these provide a sophisticated background for any modern arrangement and with a little care they will last indefinitely. (See Illustration 14.)

Sea Grape is a southern tree which grows particularly in Florida. It has a dense and spreading shape with oval green leaves strikingly veined in bright red. These leaves are wonderful for drying since they retain their heavy stiff texture. The younger ones, of 2″ to 3″, dry chartreuse while older leaves of 6″ to 8″ turn a luggage tan. The veining in the leaf does not retain its color when dried but it remains prominent. Sea Grape leaves have become so popular that dried ones can be obtained at any store specializing in dried plants.

Croton is one of the most colorful of foliage plants with endless variety in its profusion of leaves. Some are broad, others narrow and still others twist and curl into fascinating shapes. If they are processed when the color in the leaf is brilliant, they will retain much of their vividness. Those of green and white combinations usually dry with both colors clearly defined.

Orchid leaves are usually overlooked in admiration of the magnificent flower yet the long slender leaf is marvelous for drying. Lay the leaves on an absorbent paper in a dry spot and they will assume pleasing shapes and colors

14. EXOTIC MODERN

A Fiberglas dish on a wrought-iron trivet holds this modern design in brown and tan composed of Cycus (shaped before drying), Okra, Traveler's-Tree pods, Paulownia pods and Sea Grape leaves.

Robert Scharff

as the moisture gradually disappears. It may take several months for them to become completely dry. Orchid leaves keep their original leathery quality, giving them a distinctive character and stamina enough for repeated use. The fat, stubby stem which normally holds the food reserve for the plant may also be dried. They may be left on the leaf or dried separately.

FLORIST FOLIAGES

Today, most florists stock a variety of foliages for their customers. It is wise to know what is available and take advantage of these for drying. Eucalyptus, Galax, Lemon, Leucothoë and Magnolia are usually on hand but some of these and other rare leaves may have to be ordered in advance.

Lemon leaves, despite the common name, are not from a tree but a shrub, Shallon. The dark green leaves, 3″ to 5″ long, have a leathery quality and when dried turn a silvery gray-green. This is one of the easiest foliages to dry and is extremely useful in decorative work.

Eucalyptus, because of its innumerable species, has many sizes and shapes among its leaves. The tough leathery quality found in the Lance, Flat or Spiral types is well suited to drying and ideal for glycerine treatment. This is one of the pleasantest foliages to handle since its pungent aroma lasts after it is dried.

The leaves of the flat Eucalyptus can be fashioned into attractive flower forms. While they are fresh, strip the leaves from the stem and push a fine wire through the base of each leaf. Bring the ends of the wires together and twist to form a stem 5″ to 6″ long. To make a flower shape, 15 to 20 wired leaves will be needed. In the beginning, group the smaller ones in your hand for the center portion of the flower form and add the larger ones lower on the outside. Wrap corsage tape tightly about all the grouped wire stems to hold them in place. Hang the rosettes of leaves to dry. The size can be large or small and a group of 2 or 3 adds distinction to an arrangement.

CHART 5. SOME FOLIAGES SUITED TO DRYING

This chart gives the names of some leaves which have been dried successfully. The numbers in the method column correspond to the numbers given to drying methods described in this chapter and indicate the one to be used for best results.

NAME	SHAPE	PROCESSED	METHOD	COLOR WHEN DRIED
ACACIA, *Acacia decurrens*	feathery	stem	2	gray-green
ALMOND, TROPICAL or INDIAN, *Terminalia catappa*	large oval	singly	1, 3	rich red-brown
ANTHURIUM, *Anthurium veitchii*	oblong	singly	1, 2, 3, 5	tan, green
ARTEMISIA (Wormwood), (Silver King), *Artemisia albula*	feathery	stem	2	gray
ASPIDISTRA, *Aspidistra elatior*	glossy, long	singly	1, 2, 3	light brown
BEECH, EUROPEAN, *Fagus sylvatica*	lobed ovate	stem	1, 5	green
BIRD-OF-PARADISE FLOWER, *Strelitzia*	large, long	singly	1, 2, 3	green, tan
CALLA LILY, *Zantedeschia aethiopica*	arrowhead	singly	1, 2, 4	tan

SOME FOLIAGES SUITED TO DRYING (*Cont.*)

Name	Shape	Processed	Method	Color When Dried
CANNA, *Canna generalis*, garden types	large, long	singly	1, 2, 3	green, brown
CASTOR-OIL PLANT (Palma Christi), *Ricinus communis*	many-lobed	singly	1, 3, 4	red to brown
CAT'S-EAR, *Hypochaeris radicata*	lobed, hairy	singly	1	white
CATTAIL (Reed), *Typha*	long, slender	singly	1, 2	tan
CECROPIA (Snakewood Tree), *Cecropia palmata*	7-11 lobes	singly	2, 3	brown top, creamy bottom
CORN (Maize), *Zea mays*	long, wide	singly	1, 2	tan, brown, green
COTTONWOOD, *Populus balsamifera*	heart	singly	1, 2	green, tan
CROTON, *Codiaeum*	long or lobed	singly	1, 2, 4	all colors
CYCAS, *Cycas*	long, pinnate	singly	1, 2	green, tan
DRACAENA, *Dracaena*	long, broad	singly	1, 2, 5	dark brown, green
DUSTY MILLER, *Senecio cineraria*	soft, wooly	bunch	1, 2	gray
EUCALYPTUS (Gum Tree), *Eucalyptus*	varied	stem	1, 3	blue-green

Name	Leaf shape	Arrangement	Number	Color
FERNS, native varieties	various	single frond	1	green, tan
GALAX, *Galax aphylla*	heart	singly	1, 5	brown, green
GERANIUM (Storksbill), *Pelargonium*	deeply cut	singly	1, 2	green, tan
GLADIOLUS	sword	singly	1, 2, 3	tan
HORSE CHESTNUT, *Aesculus hippocastanum*	5-7 leaflets	singly	1, 2	tan, green
IRIS	sword	singly	1, 2	tan
IVY, ENGLISH, *Hedera helix*	3-5-lobed	singly	1, 5	dark green
LEMON (Salal), *Gaultheria shallon*	oval	branch	1, 2, 5	gray-green
LOTUS, *Nelumbium*	circular	singly	1, 2, 5	gray-green
MAGNOLIA (Bull Bay), *Magnolia grandiflora*	oval	singly	1, 2, 5	green top, brown bottom
MAPLE, JAPANESE, *Acer palmatum*	lobed, divided	branch	1, 5	scarlet
RED, *Acer rubrum*	lobed	branch	1, 5	green, red
NORWAY, *Acer platanoides*	lobed	branch	1, 5	green, yellow
MULLEIN, *Verbascum thapsus*	wooly, oblong	singly	1, 2	gray
OAK, WHITE, *Quercus alba*	lobed	branch	1, 2, 5	green or autumn colors
SCARLET, *Quercus coccinea*	lobed	branch	1, 2, 5	green or autumn colors

SOME FOLIAGES SUITED TO DRYING (Cont.)

NAME	SHAPE	PROCESSED	METHOD	COLOR WHEN DRIED
OAK (Cont.)				
SCRUB, *Quercus ilicifolia*	lobed	branch	1, 2, 5	green or autumn colors
BLACK, *Quercus velutina*	lobed	branch	1, 2, 5	green or autumn colors
ORCHID, cattleya, cymbidium, cypripedium types	long	singly	3	tan
PALM, *Sabal palmetto*	compounded	singly	2	gray-green
PEONY, *Paeonia*	compounded	singly	1, 2	tan, green
PERUVIAN DAFFODIL, *Ismene calathina*	long	singly	1, 2, 3	tan, green
PLANTAIN LILY, *Hosta*	broad, ovate	singly	1, 4	tan, green
RHODODENDRON (Rosebay)	oblong	singly	1, 2	green
RUBBER PLANT, *Ficus elastica*	thick, oblong	singly	1, 3, 4	light tan
RASPBERRY (Brambles), *Rubus idaeus*	toothed	stem	1	green top, white bottom
SASSAFRAS, *S. variifolium*	1-3-lobed	singly	1, 2	tan

SEA GRAPE, *Coccolobis uvifera*	orbicular	singly	1, 3	chartreuse, tan
SILVER TREE, *Leucadendron argenteum*	lanceolate	bunch	2	silvery gray
SWEET GUM, *Liquidambar styraciflua*	star	singly	1, 5	tan, green, yellow
SWEET PEA, *Lathyrus odoratus*	linear	stem	1	light green
TI, CORDYLINE, *Dracaena terminalis*	long, pointed	singly	1, 3	tan, green
WOOLY LAMB'S-EAR, *Stachys lanata*	wooly, oblong	singly	1, 2	gray
YUCCA (Adam's Needle), *Yucca filamentosa*	sword	singly	1, 2	gray-green

How to Use

8. Arranging Dried Plants

Arrangements of plant materials can no longer be considered as a luxury or the hobby of a few; they have become a part of our culture. It is as important for the modern homemaker to know how to make pleasing and harmonious floral decorations for her home as it is to balance her household budget or plan a successful party menu. There never has been and never will be a charming room without plants; therefore, an understanding of the decorative value of dried plants is a valuable part of household knowledge.

Arrangements for the home do not have to be expensive or highly stylized. Their sole purpose is to give beauty and a simple, colorful grouping of dried plants reflects as much beauty as a dozen roses. Dramatic, exotic compositions are fun to admire at an exhibition but they are neither restful nor satisfying to live with. Home arrangements are not as exacting as those created for a flower show where they will be judged for their technical accuracy. Don't be afraid to display your concept of beauty with dried plants even if you have no precedent for it.

The art of arranging plants is not a modern idea, but goes back to the sixth century B.C., when the Buddhist priests were the first people known to fix cut plants into designs before their altars. The Japanese developed flower arranging into a decorative art and the teachings of their numerous schools have influenced floral design throughout the world. We who arrange plants today, borrow ideas from the East, such as purity of line and subtle balance, and, adding our love of color, create distinctive artistic arrangements to beautify our homes.

Current decorating trends, too, borrow ideas from many eras and places. We have developed the faculty of blending period pieces, and objects from many lands, with today's furniture in a way that adds up to a smart interior. Such combinations have created a twentieth-century style called Contemporary, i.e., what we use today.

Contemporary arrangements of dried plants also mix and blend ideas. They are an American form of art and are the most satisfying of all designs for present-day homes. We approach arranging in a refreshing, new way, by using all kinds of dried plants regardless of their nature. We are not bound by tradition to certain seasonal combinations, like the Orientals, so we use native plants with tropical ones, vegetables with greenhouse plants, and dried with fresh. This type of arrangement lends itself to many kinds of home settings.

Do not jump to the conclusion that Contemporary arrangements are confused or disorganized. If you study a few, you will realize that each one, though it shows freedom and imagination, is built on a well-thought-out plan. Designs combine line and mass with each dried plant selected to form a definite part of the composition. (Illustration 15.)

Often a figurine or other ceramic object is included in the arrangement's design. Ceramics have achieved popularity in recent years and you will find unusual pieces in shops about your town. Another favorite idea is to make the composition directly on a stand, base or mat with no apparent container.

You make a dried arrangement in the same way as you make any other type of arrangement. There is nothing difficult or tricky about it. You are creating a picture and if you think of it in that fashion you will unconsciously apply the basic principles of design to your arrangements. Many of the so-called rules of arrangement are natural expressions of good taste and discrimination which you follow instinctively.

If you find it difficult to know where to find ideas or inspiration, observe the things about you. The growth of plants is a wonderful source of ideas. Often the lines or shape of a dried plant itself will suggest a design. I have derived unusual color combinations from looking at magazine advertisements. The new automobiles could inspire a modern streamlined design. Any creative work starts with an idea.

Successful arrangements must be properly composed, proportionally balanced and harmoniously grouped. Every arrangement should have a logical plan for relating the

15. CONTEMPORARY

A base of old brass holds this design showing the present-day use of line and mass. The Smoke-bush branches, Siberian Iris pods and Beech leaves are tan while the Yarrow and Marigold shade from light-yellow to deep-orange.

Robert Scharff

Robert Scharff

16. LILLIPUTIAN

This small-scale arrange-ment includes grasses and Sweet Pea vine leaves dried green with Columbine and Dictam-nus pods dried tan in a green pottery container.

component parts of the design to one another and each part to the finished whole. The container, to some extent, will govern the shape, form and style of the plan.

Proportional balance is concerned with the placement of various parts of a design in relation to the central axis. If this axis, which may be actual or imaginary, is at the center, a design will look stable and never seem inclined to tip either way. Balance may be symmetrical or asymmetrical. In a symmetrical design, you place similar pieces on both sides of the axis of the arrangement. In asymmetrical designs, the two sides may be different, but each should have the same visual weight. This latter type of balance is often used in decorating. For example, when a vase is placed on one end of a mantel it is balanced by using a tray, figurine or other object, of the same visual weight, on the other end.

There should be harmony in color and texture between the dried plants of a design and the furnishings of a room. Color is a compelling element of any design and when keyed to a room adds harmoniously to the whole.

There are many theories as to the best way to make a dried arrangement. The construction of any arrangement is a matter of personal choice. I find that it is easier to start with the top of a design and work down. I like to block out an outline or skeleton upon which to build the design by placing 3 main lines, the first of which is the central axis or main high line. Suggested mechanics are discussed in Chapter 9. The famous formula of making the high line one and a half times the height of a tall container or the width of a low one, is a safe principle to follow. Frequently I use more height in the main vertical line because it looks better and gives the finished arrangement greater dignity.

If my design is to be one of symmetrical balance, such as a fan, the second and third lines are placed on either side of the main axis at equal points half way down its length. But if I plan a design of asymmetrical balance, the second line is cut to half the length of the first and placed at one side. The third line is cut to half the length of the second and placed on the other side. This roughs out a framework which by subsequent placement of plants can develop into a triangle, oval or semicircle. Many dried plants tend naturally to fall into designs of triangular or circular shapes and they never become monotonous if you vary colors, plants and combinations.

When the outline is made you begin putting in the secondary placement of plants. These should emphasize the first and form an intermediary transition to the lower portion of the design. A large form, or group of smaller ones, strategically placed in a design unites the whole with a center of interest. When you dry plants with artistic shapes of your choice, let them be the elements of your next design.

Design is important in dried arrangements and it pays to spend time in perfecting one. Some of the most frequently used patterns are crescent, hogarth (S-curve), fan, triangle, round, oval, U-shaped, vertical, pyramid and horizontal.

The crescent is a graceful design with many variations. The half-moon outline can be made with curved stems, branches or leaves. The main top line and the lower one, arranged at either side of a container, should curve inward to give the shape. Low or shallow containers are excellent for this type of design. Once the form is set any number of dried plants can be added to form the mass pattern with a crescent outline.

SMALL ARRANGEMENTS

Small arrangements of dried plants are popular and becoming increasingly important as home decorative pieces. You will be delighted by the dash of color they provide on an occasional table, desk or hanging shelf. In fact, one of these gay little compositions is effective in the bedroom, kitchen and many other places all over the house.

A small arrangement should not be confused with a "miniature." The term miniature, in flower-show language, means an arrangement 5" high. In the home a height of 10" to 12" gives more opportunity for pleasing designs and greater freedom in the use of plants. (See Illustration 16.)

Dried plants lend themselves well to small arrangements because many are found with the right proportions. It should be kept in mind that although small, these arrangements follow the same principles as larger ones. The design of each should be definitely distinguishable, colorful, well balanced and scaled to size. Above all, avoid giving them the appearance of being overcrowded.

The selection of dried plants for a small design depends to a great extent on the container. Those in good scale give the best effect and part of the fun of these arrangements is in seeing how many appropriate materials you can dry.

At times you may be forced to cut plants down to fit a certain design.

For the main line of a tall design, you might use wisps of Scotch Broom, twigs or leaves and accent them with another kind of form, as you do in a larger-scale design. Small-sized flowers are pleasing in mass patterns. Acacia, Heather, Everlastings and Polyantha Roses are pleasing for such arrangements. Statice is a good and reliable material because of its size and lovely pastel colors. A colorful combination is Heather, several shades of purple Statice and small Ornamental Red Maple leaves. Smaller summer flowers like Baby's-Breath, Lantana and Globe Amaranth have many uses.

Small arrangements are a great challenge and it is fascinating to see how much variety there can be. Grasses, seed pods such as Columbine and Rose of Sharon, berries like Bittersweet and Bayberry—all are useful and one could go on endlessly with suggestions for these charming arrangements. The container for small arrangements is a most important feature and is covered fully in the next chapter.

Children love to make these arrangements and are particularly adept at fixing small designs. As all children are born imitators, this is a way to stimulate an interest in Nature and give them knowledge which may be an important part of their future lives.

9. Containers and Mechanics of Dried Arrangements

One of the most important parts of any dried arrangement is the receptacle which holds the materials. The word container is applied to this receptacle, being flexible enough to include any type of object, from an expensive vase to a sea shell. Since dried plants do not require water, the scope of containers is not as limited as it is for living plants. There are few objects into which you cannot put designs of dried plants if they are selected with taste and discrimination.

A container is something which you must have but its size, pattern, and color should never overshadow the dried plants in it. The plants themselves are the focus for attention and nothing detracts from them more than an ornate container of bright color or bold pattern.

The shape and size of a container will usually indicate the type of design best suited to it. Oval or round shapes show off circular designs while tall containers look better with plants with vertical lines. A container used on the floor to hold heavy branches or plants should be large in size and heavy in feeling, while a smaller vase or bowl is more appropriate for a dainty design to set upon a table.

Before you buy a container, visualize where you will place it and the type of plants you will use in it. It is not necessary to own a large number of containers to make designs for your home. Except for special occasions, several varieties of shapes are sufficient. Simple shapes and neutral colors can be used over and over again like a basic dress in your wardrobe. The color of a container does not have to match exactly the furnishings or plants but it should be neutral enough to blend with or complement both.

When you become a dried-plant enthusiast one of your greatest joys will be searching for unusual containers. An aspiring hobbyist can gather interesting yet inexpensive containers from many places. A country auction or an antique shop often reveals a treasure. You may run across old candle molds or quaint old lamps. Illustration 22 shows how a part of an old oil lamp can be made into an attractive container.

If you are fortunate enough to own fine old pieces of china, glass or luster, you have ideal containers. A silver luster pitcher or sugar bowl is good-looking with gray and blue, or gray and rose, dried plants. Pieces of milk-white glass or ironstone, are effective with many colored dried plants. Beautiful old pieces are a joy to handle and use and should not be left to gather dust on the shelf.

Kitchen utensils of a former era are enticing containers radiating a quaint charm. An old wooden chopping or

Adrien Boutrelle

17. RURAL HARVEST

Grandmother's wooden cutlery box (with hooks added for legs) holds this arrangement combining dried cornstalks and tassels, grains, corn and walnuts with fresh Leucothoë foliage, Squash, Pears and two kinds of Grapes.

butter bowl, cheese box or mortar is perfectly suited to a design of dried plants. Illustration 17 shows an old family cutlery box which was converted into a container by attaching closet hooks for supporting feet. The soft color and texture of antique earthenware jars, crocks and jugs, can be used to emphasize dried plants.

Baskets have always been important as containers for household needs. The early settlers found them indispensable and in the legacy of objects from the early days we find many unusual examples of their craft. Present-day shops, to meet the demands of the modern housewife, display styles of baskets to meet every need. Many of these are ingeniously designed and admirably suited to dried arrangements. You can make a charming arrangement in a garden basket. The round or oblong European bread basket is an inexpensive container. The baskets from the Orient, with their unusual shapes, workmanship, colors and textures are also worth seeking.

Present-day kitchen utensils are also suited to designs of dried plants. The gleam of copper forms an interesting contrast to the textures of dried plants. There are attractive shapes in mugs, pitchers, casseroles and canisters. Modern earthenware casseroles, with their simple lines and subtle tone finishes are also suitable as containers. Plastic kitchenware, now available in pastel colors, is useful for informal designs.

Other metals like brass, pewter, iron, aluminum or bronze, make compatible containers. Pewter pieces blend with colored or gray-toned plants. A piece of black iron, such as an old stove top or a modern wrought-iron tray,

Robert Schar

18. CONTAINERS

This selection of containers, all suitable for holding arrangements of dried materials, gives some idea of the large variety now available.

is suitable. A bronze container is always a treasure to have and use.

American potters are making containers, vases and bowls of every shape and style for every taste and occasion. Many are copies of ancient designs since classic shapes are suited to contemporary ideas of decoration. The ornate vase or bowl of yesteryear is rapidly being replaced by containers of neutral color, simple lines and soft texture. No longer are we content to put dried plants into any receptacle regardless of its compatibility. Styles change in containers just as they do in clothes. While the smart container of several years ago was the Chinese pillow type (resembling a large brick set on one end with the other hollowed out) today, the trend favors classic urns or footed shapes. In selecting any container much depends on personal taste and furnishings.

When you wish an unusual container for your dried plants, think about the use of a natural form for this purpose. The sculpturesque form of a shell or a piece of coral has possibilities for a novel design. A piece of fungus with an interesting shape and markings is particularly adaptable as a container. The natural beauty in wood forms and their uses as containers are mentioned in Chapter 12.

For small dried arrangements you have fascinating possibilities. The contents of your cupboard may reveal many potential containers—a footed sherbet or goblet is ideal for a small mass bouquet; ashtrays have great possibilities; colorful small pieces of glass, pottery or china are often delightful. White goes with practically any décor and small pieces of milk glass look well on dark or light furniture. A small lacquer box, perfume bottle or sea shell would be a perfect container.

BASES AND STANDS

Any object placed under a container as a stand or base becomes a part of it. A well-chosen stand will enhance the appearance of a container and add a feeling of dignity and balance. How great the difference may be is hard to visualize until an appropriate one has been tried. Many containers, especially those of Oriental manufacture, have a stand designed as an integral part of the container.

In each instance, the right stand presents an individual problem and its selection is not always an easy matter. A stand or base is always subordinate to a container and its proportions should be relative to those of the container. An oblong or rectangular base improves the appearance of a tall container, while an oval or round shape is more effective to set off a round dish. Simple shapes of attractively finished wood will increase the artistic effect of any container.

Although we think primarily of wood as the material for stands, often a dining-table mat of straw, matting or natural fiber, is used for a dried-plant design. A raft (short lengths of thin bamboo lashed together) is a popular base for dried plants. Often a design of dried plants is placed directly on the raft with no visible container to produce an unusual effect.

MECHANICS

When you look at a dried arrangement all you see is the appeal and beauty of the design, but behind this lies another important element: mechanics. Mechanics are the devices and techniques which are employed to accomplish a desired result. A little know-how will enable you to conceal cleverly any device so it is never so obvious as to spoil an arrangement. The techniques and devices for dried plants differ somewhat from those used with fresh plants, where an adequate supply of water is necessary.

If you have ever worked with dried plants, you know

how obstinate they can be about staying in place. This is where mechanics come to your aid. Control of plants is essential for pleasure in their use and the simplest of gadgets will stabilize dried designs.

I have found that it saves time and makes arrangements much more fun if all the mechanical equipment is kept in one easily available place. A box or basket will be sufficient for the average homemaker but an enthusiastic hobbyist will devote a closet or a room to containers and equipment. The following items for use with dried plant materials are simple and none of the articles are expensive. Many can be acquired at the dime store.

Holders. The most popular holder is the lead-based needlepoint one. The base is strong; the spikes close enough to hold either large or small stems; and the shapes varied. Some have interlocking bases which may be used together or separately. If the weight in the base is not sufficient to hold heavy plants, the holder can be anchored with melted paraffin or clay.

Since colonial times, sand has held dried-plant designs and packing vases with sand is still a popular practice. However, unless reinforced, some plant stems break easily when inserted, and if the sand slips or slides, the design does likewise. Vermiculite in a container acts in the same fashion.

Another useful medium for holding dried plants is clay and it may be molded to correspond with the size of a container. The clay should have a heavy consistency, like Plasticine (not children's modeling clay), to hold dried plants adequately. One may start the opening in a block of clay with a sharp point, then insert the stem and firmly mold the clay about it.

In containers with a wide opening a crumpled ball of 2″-mesh chicken wire is an excellent holder. It can be shaped to the size of a container, thus allowing stems to be inserted at any angle. If you pour 2″ or 3″ of sand into a deep container and add the wire, stems may be pressed through the wire openings into the sand for anchorage.

Styrofoam, a plastic, provides the simplest way for designs to stay unalterably in place. It has replaced many other types of holders in my arrangements. It is easy to obtain, inexpensive, clean to handle and does not deteriorate.

With a wet knife, plastic foam can be cut to fit any container. For example: fill a tall container three-fourths full with sand and cut a piece of foam to fit on top thus allowing the use of much shorter stems. In a shallow dish, foam may be used by pouring a thin layer of paraffin into the container and placing the foam on it. When the paraffin hardens, you have a firm holder.

If the perfection of an arrangement in a low or shallow dish is not to suffer, it will be necessary to conceal the holder. You can easily hide it with a few pretty stones, clinkers, rock formations, colored marbles, or chips of colored glass. Shale has lovely colors and can easily be broken into pieces suitable for a covering.

Securing and Supporting Items.   Many dried stems are too weak or brittle to be used without some reinforcement.

Toothpicks, florist sticks or pipe cleaners lengthen and strengthen stems and may be attached with raffia, Twistems (patented plant ties) or florist tape. Sometimes a splint is necessary to rescue a broken stem and wrapping both stem and stick with brown or green florist corsage tape makes it less noticeable. Pipe cleaners are dependable for strengthening stems and at the same time allow them to be bent into a desired curve or line. Wire, unless extremely fine and carefully used, tears the stems of dried plants. Twistems are better since the wire is encased in a protective plastic covering.

As you progress in the art of arranging dried plants you will devise still other aids. An emergency will spark ingenious ideas to cope with the situation. Such things as chewing gum and hairpins can be indispensable as props and on several occasions have saved the life of an arrangement.

Stability is essential in dried arrangements. Each piece of the design should be firmly anchored in place. A good firm start can be made by attaching the first, taller pieces of a design to a dowel pin, ¼" in diameter, and cleverly concealing it among the plants. Once it is firmly anchored in the holder half the battle is over, and subsequent insertions will not disturb it. Elastic bands or raffia are excellent for tying small or thin stems into groups to avoid the frustration of trying to insert each stem separately.

GROOMING OF DRIED PLANTS

Dried arrangements should be kept fresh and crisp by good grooming. Any broken, faded flowers or leaves should be removed from a design and replaced with fresh ones.

A small, soft, moistened brush can be used to whisk dust from plants, and foliage may be wiped with a damp cloth or moistened cotton pad. Many kinds of tropical plants can be washed without harm.

Do not hesitate to treat dried plants. Anything is permissible if it does not make the materials look unnatural. Fresh leaves can be wiped with an oil to give them a sheen and shoe polish adds a luster to dried ones. The leaf's texture must be sturdy and firm to withstand the application of polish which produces pleasing highlights although it does change color slightly. Choose brown polish for brown leaves, oxblood or neutral for others.

Liquefied plastics in a can with a spray attachment can be used to lengthen the life of some dried plants and revitalize others which show signs of wear. For example a burry pod, like those of the Castor Bean, will remain crisp with a plastic coating. This colorless film is excellent to preserve the silken tufts in a half-open Milkweed pod. Plastic spray improves some dried flowers and leaves but impairs others. Personal experiments have shown that Celosia is marred, while Pearly Everlasting remains white and Goldenrod does not break apart after a coating. Magnolia and Shallon are improved with a coating, while leaves with a soft, dull appearance, like Canna, are better left natural. A coating makes a dried Artichoke more attractive, but spoils the woody texture of cones.

When a clear plastic spray is not available, you will find that hair-net spray is an adequate substitute. It produces the same results and its lightly perfumed odor is a pleasing substitute for floral fragrance.

10. Period Designs of Dried Plants

The furnishings of many homes have been inspired by such historical periods of decoration as early American or Victorian. Houses are seldom exact reproductions of those in a former era because, to be in keeping with the times in which we live, modern conveniences undreamed of by our ancestors are included. Many people are turning back to the traditional and find that, by using family treasures or acquired antiques for both furnishings and household articles, they can create an atmosphere of unity and charm.

It is fascinating to adapt the floral design of a former time to dried plants. Working out a particular style for a period setting will take a little time and thought but it will prove a stimulating challenge. These arrangements should not be exact copies but merely indicate the influence of the era. Adaptations provide ample leeway for individual choice of both ideas and plants.

Designs, which we regard as typical of an era, may not always be correct since all we have to rely upon are floral decorations of the period recorded in architecture, paintings, ceramics or old books. In all parts of the country there are museums and replicas or restorations of homes and villages to supply reliable information. For example, the American Wing of the Metropolitan Museum of Art in New York houses several collections of fine old American furnishings. The best way to make compositions with a degree of authenticity is to familiarize yourself with the period and interpret its atmosphere according to your furnishings. You will find that varying quantities of plant materials were made into mass bouquets for their beauty and fragrance and that only in recent years have we had new principles to improve the decorative effect of plant compositions.

The average American homeowner is interested in furnishings that stand for some period in American history, therefore the following comments are limited to this field.

COLONIAL AMERICAN

Since America's colonies were settled by a variety of Old World peoples, it is not strange that we find echoes of varying cultures in American Colonial style. The influence of Georgian England appears in Philadelphia and Virginia; France in Charleston and the Dutch in Pennsylvania. All of these early furnishings are commonly called Colonial but we should realize that there are naturally variations in building styles and modes of furnishings.

Early American.   New England originated most of the furnishings we now speak of as Early American. The rocky soil, cold climate and Puritan way of life had a bearing on both architecture and furnishings. The early table, chest, chair or stool, was a simple, sturdy piece fashioned from natural wood by the carpenter. Typical are the Windsor or Hitchcock chair, trestle and gate-leg table, and cobbler's bench. Today, furniture of this type is used with colorful chintz or calico, hooked rugs and the gleam of pewter or brass for interesting, informal and charming homes.

The early colonists loved flowers and examples of their informal bouquets are to be found in many old volumes. In those days the ladies of the household had little leisure to devote to frivolities, therefore their arrangements were simple and unassuming. An arrangement to harmonize with Early American furniture would be a bouquet of mixed flowers, leaves and herbs, with each plant chosen for its color or fragrance and arranged somewhat as they might have been gathered in the garden. Plants were never arranged in a set pattern as we do today. You will find that the shape of one or two large flowers is often given prominence enough to dominate the whole bouquet. Sometimes the design is circular because the nosegay is typical of this era. The container which holds the bouquet should reflect the same simple, informal feeling. The plants to dry and use for an Early American arrangement are:

Garden Flowers	Columbine, Everlastings, Honesty, Marigolds, Pinks, Roses, Strawflowers, Zinnias, etc.
Wild Flowers	Goldenrod, Joe-Pye Weed, Pearly Everlasting, Queen Anne's Lace.
Herbs	Artemisia, Mint, Rosemary, Tansy, Yarrow.
Other Materials	Berries (Bittersweet, Bayberry), Corn, Ferns, Grains, Grasses, Gourds, Leaves, Nuts.

Adrien Boutrelle

19. GEORGIAN COLONIAL

This formal mass design in a gold-trimmed white urn is predominantly pastel with pink and rose Snapdragons and single Peonies. Artemisia and white and rose Statice give a softening effect and Sweet Pea and Peony foliages supply the finishing touch.

Suitable containers include bean pots, baskets, ginger jars, jugs, mugs, pitchers, sugar bowls, tea pots, pieces of glass, metal containers (pieces of early design in copper, brass or pewter), wooden pieces (chopping or butter bowl, or a copy of an old wooden utensil).

Georgian Colonial.   As the colonies flourished and mere survival was no longer the greatest concern the people had time to seek beauty in their surroundings. With the development of Colonial mansions, such as those seen at Mount Vernon, Monticello or Williamsburg, there began probably the most gracious era in American history. The architecture and decorations followed the luxurious Georgian style of England and is often spoken of as Georgian Colonial.

If you visit Williamsburg during the winter months you will fully realize the value of dried plants in true period settings. For today, just as in the era of Williamsburg's glory, you will see colorful arrangements, entirely of dried plants, set upon a chest, table or under a large picture. The culture and the refinement of the people who once inhabited old Williamsburg are reflected in these arrangements, and years of research have gone into their reproduction. The eighteenth-century compositions contain many ideas which can be adapted to homes with furniture modeled after the pieces made by Sheraton, Hepplewhite, Adam or Duncan Phyfe.

All of the arrangements in Williamsburg are well-filled masses and the containers are in perfect harmony with the furnishings. The shape of the mass is either higher than wide or wider than high, and some bouquets have materials radiating like the ribs in a fan. Many arrangements

Robert Scharff

20. IN THE WILLIAMSBURG MANNER

A white five-fingered holder contains a full mass bouquet composed of Artemisia, white Everlasting, Honesty, Roses, Strawflowers, Celosia, Statice and Maple and Raspberry leaves.

have a lighter type of plant placed at the outer rim to form a soft edging to the design. The dried bouquets are composed of many pastel colors or rich deep colors. Often one color with its various values in leaves and flowers is used throughout the arrangement. Illustration 20 portrays the feeling of old Williamsburg in a modern adaptation.

Some of the plant materials which can be dried for the Georgian Colonial type of arrangement are:

Grasses	Plume, Spike, Foxtail.
Grains	Wheat, Oats, Barley.
Ferns, Seed Pods, Weeds (such as Dock).	
Leaves	Beech, Dogwood, Maple, Oak.
Wild and Garden Flowers	Globe Amaranth, Goldenrod, Honesty, Hydrangea, Joe-Pye Weed, Lantern Plant, Pearly Everlasting, Roses, Scarlet Sage, Sea Lavender, Strawflowers, Tulips.

Containers would include vases and bowls of china, pottery, pewter, glass or alabaster, also urn-shaped containers or soup tureens, glass goblets or teardrop vases. The eighteenth-century feeling can be carried out with pieces of Worcester, Lowestoft, Wedgwood and Staffordshire.

VICTORIAN

Whether you like Victorian or not it is a style which left a definite mark in the world through the volume of things it produced. Elaborate ornamentation was the essence of this nineteenth-century style and its furniture was magnificent in the use of wood. We make no pretense of following the Victorian idea of overcrowded furnishings but include some of the better pieces to convey the quaint charm of this period.

Decorative pieces of the Victorian era were heavy masses with the flowers crowded so thickly and tightly in the container that the beauty of the individual blossom was lost. They were as overstuffed as the bustle of those days. These

Adrien Boutrelle

21. VICTORIAN

A gold-trimmed antique container holds a compact mass in deep shades of red, lavender and blue with yellow and orange for contrast. Celosia, Roses, Marigolds, Daffodils, Zinnias and Hydrangeas are included in the main design and trailing artificial grapes and dried Pomegranates emphasize the Victorian feeling.

confused bouquets should not be copied but merely used as a guide in the selection of plants and containers.

Today, we interpret the era's sentiment but the massed effect is far more pleasing and less crowded. The shape may be globular or circular and the mass wider than it is high. It is not unusual to see a Victorian composition in which the height of plant materials is equal to the height of the container. There are no strict color combinations to be followed because the earlier part of the period used pastel colors while the later part favored rich, deep colors like magenta, violet and deep blue. All white arrangements were popular and this idea can be successfully adapted today. Illustration 21 shows a modern adaptation of the Victorian idea.

Many kinds of plant materials are appropriate for the Victorian style and some to be dried are:

Flowers   Celosia, Coreopsis, Dahlia, Daisy, Foxglove, Geranium, Heather, Hydrangea, Lilac, Lily, Marigold, Peony, Rose, Strawflower, Tulip and many other garden flowers. Fine dainty flowers like Baby's-Breath and Statice can be dried and used as a filler.

Other Materials   Ferns, Grains, Grasses, Herbs, Seed Pods, Thistles.

Containers. Modern copies of Victorian vases which are often better designed than their originals; flare-shaped vases; white vases with gilt ornamentation; pieces of alabaster or old Victorian silver; pieces of Victorian glass like satin, amber, cranberry, peachblow; pieces of cut or milk glass; pieces of ironstone or Parian ware; containers in which a human hand holds the vase; shells.

The Victorian glass dome was originally made to encase creations of wax or shell flowers. This craft was pursued by the ladies of that romantic era with the same enthusiasm as we do flower arranging. Since the creations were elaborate and required hours of patience and skill, they were placed under a dome of glass for safekeeping. Today a dome serves much the same purpose, allowing us to display conspicuously an arrangement of dried plants protected from dust.

MODERN

No outline of periods is complete without mentioning Modern. Although there have been attempts to apply various names, such as Progressive and Functional, to the twentieth-century style, Modern is the term in general usage. It has become international in scope with an interchange of ideas between countries and continents. Economic and social life influenced furnishings in the past and continues to influence our new materials, ideas and inventions.

Various types of Modern furnishings are used in many present-day homes varying in degree from formal to informal, modified to ultra. Modern furnishings afford a particular appeal to young people but the elimination of all but essentials often appalls the conservative older generation. Today's architecture reduces wall spaces with large windows, storage cabinets, etc. The furniture is smaller, more compact and often serves a dual purpose. Perfection of wood finish replaces ornamentation and plant arrangements should emphasize this quality. The clear-cut form of a large leaf or the exotic shape of a seed pod adds greatly to the plain surface of finely finished wood.

Modern arrangements, like other forms of modern art, break away from the traditional with a feeling of freedom. The free forms in Nature are used to make fascinating designs and often plants are manipulated or trimmed into unusual shapes. You will find that Modern arrangements have an out-of-the-ordinary design, combine color in unusual ways, and use various textures in plant materials.

Some of the plants which are suitable for drying to use in the Modern style of arrangement are:

Palm   Boot, Heart, Plume, Spade.

Leaves   Aspidistra, Canna, Croton, Dracaena, Magnolia, Sea Grape, Strelitzia, or others with bold outlines.

Pieces of Decorative Wood   Many forms and textures (see Chapter 12).

Flowers   Cockscomb, Gladiolus, Hydrangea, single Peony, wide-open Tulips, Onion Blossoms, large Zinnias, or other exotic forms.

Pods   Lotus, Poinciana, Traveler's-Tree, Yucca.

Other Plant Materials   Cactus, Cattails, Scotch Broom, and vegetables like Artichoke, Okra, etc.

Containers. A variety of Modern design pieces will serve adequately as containers and some of those from which to choose are glass blocks, Modern glass pieces (vases and bowls); pieces of aluminum, brass, copper, pewter; pieces of Modern pottery, plastics; wooden vases, bowls or trays.

Whatever period your rooms may represent, dried plants belong in them. An arrangement, in addition to being pleasing in itself must harmonize with its surroundings. Like any other of the accessories in a room, the plant design is chosen to give pleasure and reflects your concept of beauty.

The collecting and drying of plants for a period design does take time. Don't seek the impossible or go to lengths to obtain unusual or special plants since many alternates are easily obtained and will produce the same effect. You may find it necessary to dry plants from spring, summer and fall for a particular idea. The larger the mass arrangement, the more plants it requires. It is far more important to keep arrangements in your rooms throughout the year than to reserve your creative genius for an occasional exhibition.

11. Combining Dried and Fresh Plants

There are thousands of fascinating ways to combine dried plants with fresh ones. The unique qualities in these combinations are a great challenge to the imagination and you can be as reckless as you please, provided you keep within the general principles of good composition. Ten years ago it would have been deemed highly improper to mix fresh and dried plants. Today, flower arranging, no longer bound by rules and restrictions, has the greatest freedom for artistic expression.

In combining dried and fresh plants a great measure of the success lies in clever handling. You will find that, because of their diametrically different physical conditions, it is best to give prominence to either one or the other. The basic lines of a composition may be constructed of one and the other used to accent the arrangement. For example: large dried leaves are an excellent foil for fresh flowers and, in reverse, evergreens are a striking contrast to dried seed pods or cones.

One of the first needs, in combining plant materials, is a satisfactory means of keeping the stems of the fresh plants in water and the dried ones out of water. This may be done in several ways. Twin receptacles in a container is one method; another is to use a small can of water for the fresh plants and a piece of plastic foam for the dried materials. Any means may be used that is adequate, practical and easy to conceal. Dried plants may be permanently secured in a container and fresh flowers or leaves inserted at the front in a small receptacle of water, as an accent for a composition. Foliages or flowers keep fresh for days in glass or plastic orchid tubes. If you wrap the stems of dried plants with corsage tape, they may remain in water without harm.

Each season of the year offers plants which are distinctly different from those of another. It is extremely helpful if the homemaker knows what is available at each time of year and plans to use new and unusual plants each season rather than to fall back on the same old ones.

SPRING

In spring Nature brings forth her full glory of bloom. Acacia, Pansies, Tulips and Daffodils are all spring flowers which can be dried easily. Statice is always in the florist market at Easter time and it is ideal for little spring bouquets. A few sprays of freshly budded branches can be added to an arrangement to supply an inviting touch.

A joyful sight, no matter where you live, is the appear-

22. LILIES FOR EASTER

Leafless Euonymus branches and Lilies symbolize Nature's rebirth at Easter. The foliage at the base of the design is Silver Tree. The container is the lower portion of an old black iron oil lamp.

ance of the soft fuzzy catkins on the Pussy Willow because it means that winter is really over. Pussy Willows will dry excellently if the branches are cut when the catkins are about half open. The wild strains are more commonly used but the French variety has larger pink catkins.

Pussy Willows are a prime favorite for line arrangements because they can be molded to any desired shape with ease. If you wish to bend them, moisten the whole stem for a short time while fresh, and then shape it to the required line with a gentle yet firm finger-pressure. The stems will retain their new shape, when dry, if they are kept out of water.

A framework for spring arrangements can be made by shaping and drying half a dozen branches of Pussy Willows, and accenting them with freshly cut bulb materials such as Crocus, Narcissus or Tulip. There is beauty in clear line and often a small quantity of well-shaped dried plants produces a charming arrangement.

Many other spring branches lend themselves to line compositions. Wisteria with its natural twists and curls is extremely graceful. Euonymus, Viburnum, Maple and Magnolia are adequate substitutes. Sweet Gum branches grow with curves suitable for drying. Illustration 22 uses Sweet Gum branches with Easter Lilies, for a spring composition.

Spring is the time to use figurines. Many ceramic pieces give a distinct feeling of spring breezes in their flowing lines. The entire composition can be planned around one of these figures, either as part of the design or as an added accessory. Ceramic birds are symbolic of spring but rabbits, squirrels or ducks are as appropriate.

SUMMER

The lazy days of summer are not conducive to making stylized or dramatic arrangements but call for casual ones which will remain crisp no matter how high the temperature soars. Summer heat is severe on the lasting qualities of cut flowers but dried plants will survive the hottest day. Those of us who are fortunate enough to have gardens are supplied with fresh flowers all through summer which may be supplemented with dried plants.

The tall copper-brown seed heads of Dock are excellent to give proportion and style to round forms of fresh cut flowers such as Pyrethrum, Marigold, Zinnia or Gaillardia. Dried seed stalks may be substituted for Dock and wild flowers like Daisies, Black-Eyed Susan or Butterfly Weed, for garden flowers.

In summer, dried grasses have great ornamental value and their beauty lies in the graceful sweep of their stalks. Ornamental grasses are grown in many gardens and when cut and used with a few fresh flowers, it takes little else to make a simple, informal, charming arrangement. Among such grasses are the silky plumes of Pampas grasses, the fuzzy tuft of Rabbit's-Tail or the pink spikes of Cloud grasses. Grasses from swamp, field or roadside offer a wide assortment for drying. I have a special fondness for my old wooden mortar when it is arranged with dried field grasses and fresh wild Daisies and garden Cornflowers.

Most silvery gray-leaved plants dry well and those of the Artemisia family are well known. During summer, combinations of gray with blue or pink are dainty and refreshing. The gray might be supplied by dried sprays of Artemisia and leaves of Lamb's-Ear, with green, blue or pink Hydrangea.

On a hot day, green or green and white combinations provide a cool and refreshing feeling. Many seed stalks dry green and form stunning combinations with fresh-cut green and white leaves like those of Hosta. Graceful dried branches with fresh white Lilies and green and white foliage, form an unusual and lovely combination. Another refreshing idea is decorative wood with green foliage. Uses of wood are discussed in Chapter 12.

All-white arrangements are eminently suited to summer. Both fresh and dried plants can be mixed into charming bouquets, if one is careful in the choice and handling of plants. Queen Anne's Lace, Everlastings and Honesty, either dry or fresh, are indispensable for such bouquets.

FALL

In fall the fields, orchard and garden yield a rich harvest. What is more suggestive of autumn than a sheaf of grain with fruit and vegetables? Barley, Oats and Wheat are ideally suited for this use. Wheat is perhaps a little stiff, Oats are more graceful, but I like Barley best of all, because of its fascinating beard. This gives a long sweeping line to any arrangement. The grain is light in color and fruit or vegetables of a dark color give a satisfying contrast. Barley, pink Celosia and lavender grapes make a stunning combination as will yellow or orange vegetables used with Oats or Wheat.

If you want a vivid touch of color in arrangements, there is nothing better than fall foliages. The flaming red of Oak

Adrien Boutrelle

23. SEPTEMBER SONG

This arrangement of dried and fresh materials is made in
fall colors that correspond to the rooster's coloring and
includes brown Dock and cones, tan Okra pods, yellow
Squash, Yarrow and Marigold, and green Grapes and
leaves.

and Maple leaves is characteristic and many other tree foliages turn yellow and orange. Colorful foliage is not restricted to trees for the leaves of garden plants also turn color in early fall. Peony foliages turn wonderful colors. The method of drying these foliages is discussed in Chapter 7 and with a little care in selection you can dry many shades for your arrangements.

Figurines were mentioned for use in spring, but certain pieces are adaptable to fall. Any object conveying the seasonal feeling may be correlated into an arrangement. Illustration 23 is a combination of fresh and dried plants with a rooster as its accessory. The introduction of Pheasant, Turkey or Quail feathers emphasizes the seasonal motif in an unusual way. If you have a hunter in the family he will supply these or they may be obtained in a millinery supply store.

Each year I do at least one arrangement in an old straw hat! Placed on its side, with the plant materials arranged to spill and overflow from the crown's opening, it makes an unusual container. The composition usually consists of numerous kinds of fresh and dried plants. The dried ones include Grain, Corn, Gourds, Strawflowers and Celosia and the fresh include Foliage, Berries, Grapes, or other fresh fruits. When all of these various types of plants are combined in one arrangement, they should not be piled into a heterogeneous mass but carefully placed in a distinct pattern. By using closely related colors the arrangement gives a feeling of unity. This is a wonderful way to express the harvest idea at Thanksgiving. Other fall combinations are discussed in Chapter 16.

A sizable dried Gourd, with its mellow tone, is an ideal container for both dried and fresh plants in fall. A narrow slit is made in the long side of a Gourd and the seed scooped out to make a container. A small saw may be needed to cut the hard shell of a Gourd. If fresh plants are used, a small receptacle for water is inserted into the opening. When two Gourds, one larger than the other, are placed side by side and slightly offset, they form a distinctive, graduated unit.

WINTER

In winter, we use fresh flowers from the florist but a supply of dried plant materials can be the backbone of semipermanent arrangements. The totally different textures of fresh flowers are a pleasing contrast to dried plants. Two or three normal-sized flowers are sufficient to accent an arrangement. White flowers against dark materials give the illusion of black and white, while colored flowers will harmonize or contrast. Pink is pleasing against brown or gray dried plants. Gardenias or Camellias with exotic or tropical dried plants form a glamorous arrangement.

Evergreen branches are excellent as the basis of combination arrangements. Cedar, Pine and Yew are available at any season, even in the colder parts of our country. There are varied colors in the narrow, needlelike foliages of evergreens and they provide an excellent background for a mass of dried plants. Cones are attractive with Pine branches and Wood Roses with branches of golden-tipped Arborvitae.

In winter, snips from house plants, such as a few Be-

24. TROPICAL FLAVOR

A bamboo container on a large irregular-shaped stand sets a tropical note which is carried out in green and brown plant material. Here dried Canna, glycerinized Galax, Magnolia leaves and bunched Chestnuts supply tones of brown, while fresh Ti leaves, Artichokes and Grapes provide various shades of green.

gonia leaves, a trail of Pothos or Ivy, supply a fresh note to dried arrangements. When the stems are inserted in small tubes of water, and the tubes are hidden away in the dried plants, they will last for weeks. For this use green foliages, like Lemon, Leucothoë, Rhododendron or Loquat, have many desirable traits. The strong design and glossy surface of Tropical Magnolia leaves provide a contrast to brown dried materials.

Many succulents have beautifully colored rosettes of leaves and nothing more is needed to add a distinctive touch to a dried arrangement. Echeveria is one of the best due to its exquisite colors and lasting quality. It will remain in good condition, with or without water, for weeks.

In winter, fruit adds pep to dried arrangements. Lemons, Limes, Oranges or Kumquats are available in fruit markets and a grouping of their bright forms supplies color to an arrangement. Kumquats can be fashioned into bunches and used as orange-colored grapes. A fresh Pineapple blends with dried plants, especially tropical ones.

There are times when unusual objects will add a finishing touch to a dried arrangement. A flower arranger is wise to collect a few adaptable pieces, such as a group of oddly shaped colored stones, a piece of obsidian or quartz. Chunks of colored glass, broken into irregular-shaped pieces, are also popular.

Winter is the time to use the most colorful dried flowers which will bring a cheerful note to a room. After one use, many have stamina enough to be retired for a while or used in a brand-new combination. Dried flowers are a great blessing to tide us over the dark months until spring.

12. Decorative Wood

The twentieth-century has seen many changes in decorative ideas and today a natural piece of wood is the smart thing to use for home décor. People who feel that dried wood is only suitable for modern homes fail to realize that Nature's own handiwork has endless decorative possibilities.

All wood dried for decorative use is referred to as driftwood and the name implies that the wood came from beach or shore. Since wonderful pieces can be found in other places and since many parts of plants (such as the trunk, branch, twig, bark or root), when dried and regardless of where they are found, are classed as driftwood, *decorative* is a far more appropriate word than *drift*, to describe this wood.

Sun and wind do wonderful things to salt-water-soaked wood. But good, interesting pieces of actual driftwood are often hard to find at the seashore except in remote or unpopulated areas. With the present demand for decorative wood, other places must be explored.

Along a country road or in a wooded area you will see trees which have been cut and left untouched or trees which have been felled by a severe storm. Sun, wind and rain act as curing agents on the lifeless trees and turn broken parts into decorative wood of beautiful color. Valuable branches or roots lie beside the road and the average motorist passes them by without a glance. In your own vicinity there may be a beautiful piece and you should investigate the possibilities.

Many lakes have wooded areas close to their shores, and, in a dry season when the lake level is low, branches or roots become visible which otherwise are hidden. You will find that these normally submerged pieces are satiny smooth and often their artistic shape is a sheer delight.

Along the banks of a stream you may find interesting woods. One of my favorite pieces came from a brook in the rolling hills of New England. One summer my daughter and I were following the winding trail along the bank when we came upon several trees which had fallen across the brook. One piece of a tree had broken into a most artistic shape with a blue-gray color and smooth finish that would be hard to duplicate by artificial means. In trying to dislodge it my daughter was a surprised young lady when her foot slipped on a mossy rock and she found herself sitting in the shallow brook! We were a tired, wet, but jubilant pair when we arrived home with this lovely acquisition. This wood piece has had many uses both at home

25. CONTRASTING TEXTURES

For contrast in tone and texture Porcupine pods and glycerinized Magnolia leaves are grouped at the base of a smooth, bare branch of Manzanita fastened to a waxed Cedar shake.

and in exhibitions where it has earned several blue ribbons.

In every part of our country you will find pieces of wood that can be adapted to decorative ideas. Native to the West Coast, Manzanita is a large and bushy shrub with crooked branches and roots that twist and curl into unusual lines and shapes. Professional decorators have long recognized the value of these remarkable branches. (See Illustration 25.)

Cypress Knee is another interesting decorative wood found in our Southern regions. The American Cypress grows in water with 6 or 8 "knees" radiating from the trunk of the tree and rising above the water at a short distance from the tree. Botanists think these knees are used for respiration and to carry oxygen into the roots beneath the water. The size of a knee varies and it may rise several feet in height. Knees are easy to handle because they are light in weight and almost indestructible. For commercial sale, they are peeled and polished, but those which still have their natural tan bark are very good-looking.

Pieces of wood from plants in a desert area have strange shapes, so unusual as to stimulate your imagination. The arid climate and excessive heat produce a petrified or bleached wood which is excellent for decorative use.

In many areas of our country there are trees whose branches are curved by the wind. If the wind blows strongly from one direction, the tree cannot maintain its normal growth and so bends with the wind. Especially in mountainous regions, winds toss and turn the limbs of a tree until they assume fascinating shapes. Pieces so sculpted by wind can be of the greatest value.

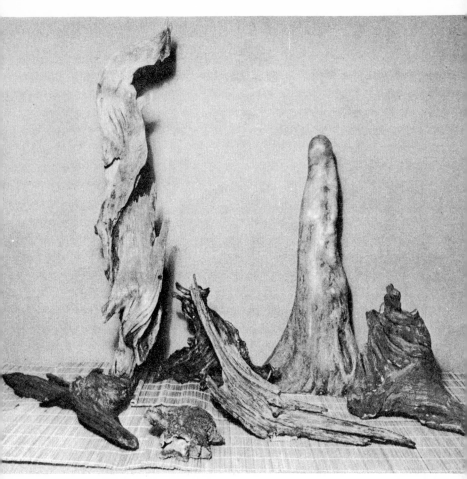

26. DECORATIVE WOODS

Despite their strong resemblance to "driftwood," not one of these wood pieces came from the seashore—they were all found in various inland places.

In California, the branches of the Monterey Cypress are twisted into grotesque shapes by the strong winds from the Pacific. There is a wonderful weather-beaten look about these Cypress branches, many of which sprawl on the ground.

If you are not of an adventurous nature or do not enjoy the thrill of searching for a treasure, wood can be purchased. Florist or speciality shops have unusual displays. Wood pieces may also be ordered by mail from advertisements found in the classified sections of magazines. Tropical-fish stores are other places to try—many lovely pieces are seen in their window or shop displays. The demand for decorative wood is such that pieces are now appearing even on the counters of roadside markets.

CONDITIONING OF WOOD

When you go in search of wood, visualize how the shape of the piece will look in the setting you plan. Is the line graceful and is its size appropriate? The physical condition of the wood itself is also important. It should be firm and hard to the touch. I like to rap a piece smartly to be sure it will not break. Generally the elements have cured wood satisfactorily, but if disintegration has set it, it may crumble at a touch.

In conditioning wood the first step is to eliminate all dirt and loose particles by giving it a good scrubbing with a stiff brush and soap and water. Possibly a second scrubbing may be necessary before it is clean enough to handle. Any decayed part may be removed by a paring knife or screw driver. The wood will require at least a week to dry or, if you wish, may be aged for a longer period. In summer, it may be left out of doors to cure.

If the surface of the wood is rough it can be smoothed with fine sandpaper or steel wool, but this should be done lightly. A coat of shellac will protect the wood fibers and also act as a filler. If the dry shellac is rubbed with a fine sandpaper it is hardly noticeable. Two coats of shellac on the underside of the wood is a practical protection.

My personal preference is to leave the exposed surface of a wood piece natural because the grain and color have a charm which is hard to improve upon. However, in certain instances, artificial treatment does bring out qualities which may not have been naturally evident in the wood. Wood is often waxed, varnished, tinted or stained. There are many other ways to treat wood and anything from shoe polish to bleach may be used to give a desired result. I like to apply a little color to some wood by rubbing a small amount of well-thinned paint into it with a cloth or, better still, with my fingers. The lights and shadows of the grain are followed and the color varied accordingly, to keep the wood's natural beauty. White, gray or brown paints are best, as they can be made nearly the color of the wood.

WOOD ARRANGEMENTS

To make a piece of wood distinctive in an arrangement, its shape and natural traits should be emphasized. A curve is easy to exaggerate if you add other plant material in the same general line. A long sweeping branch is given balance by a grouping of material at its base. Sometimes several branches fitted together are a more satisfying shape than one by itself. It is amazing how different a branch may look when turned at various angles. A simple piece of wood may be used in a dozen different ways, and space allows me to mention only a few.

Many shapes of wood are suitable for mounting on a board or a piece of Masonite. A good formation may be set upright and fastened at its base by a screw up through the board and into the wood itself. The base of the wood may have to be sawed to achieve the proper mounting angle or bevel for maximum effect. Once a piece of wood is permanently set in its base, it will suggest numerous arranging ideas.

Placing plant materials on the coffee table is popular and one of our neighbors uses an exceptionally formed piece of wood to spotlight her large table. The wood is permanently mounted, and its color and size blend perfectly with the table top. Each season a few timely pieces of fresh plant material from her garden are added for a decorative touch.

Another shape in wood may be used more appropriately in a container or as background for other plant materials. Metal and pottery containers are good choices for this purpose because wood usually looks best in a container which is sturdy and neutral in color.

In some pieces of wood you will find crevices or small openings in which a receptacle can be hidden. If perishable plant materials are used in the design, here is the place for a water container to keep them fresh. The size of the opening will determine the kind of a receptacle which can

be used, but test or orchid tubes, small cans, jelly glasses or bottles are usually suitable. At times a custard cup or a baby-food jar can solve the problem. Several chunks of clay or strips of Scotch tape are usually all the fastening required to hold such containers in place.

When a shape of wood is long and narrow and has a graceful outline, it may be placed in a horizontal position on a table to serve as a container for fruits and vegetables. For summer meals served out of doors a wood piece makes an excellent table motif because its sturdy character resists a wind or breeze. When luscious fruits, like large bunches of grapes, are artistically fixed upon a wood piece, the result is not only decorative but tempting to the appetite. Highly polished apples or mellow peaches, plus a few sprays of foliage, are eye-appealing. These are ideas quickly executed and simple enough to please the busiest housekeeper.

An unusual piece of wood can be made into the base for a lamp to be used in the sun room, game room or living room. Wood has an air of informality that is in tune with the tempo of relaxed living in these rooms. Another clever way to use wood is to let a tree stump support a table top made of another piece of wood or glass.

There is no end to the versatility of wood. A little know-how is all that it takes to create an individual idea and you would do well to consider a wood piece for your home.

27. STICKS AND STONES

Here two pieces of wood form a container for a design featuring Scotch Broom in the background with rust-colored Chrysanthemums, Ivy leaves and a few stones at the base.

obert Scharff

13. Flower Prints

Flower prints are pictures created with colorful, pressed dried plants. They are a charming and appealing form of artistic expression. You will find it fascinating to use colorful pressed flowers to create pictures for the walls of your home. Decorating with flower pictures is in vogue today, and prints of real flowers furnish a delightful accent to any interior.

Many Botanical Gardens, Natural History Museums and universities have collections of pressed dried plants for reference and study. Such a collection is called an herbarium and each plant in it is pressed, dried, mounted and accurately labeled for the student of botany. The method of pressing plants for an herbarium is not very different from the one used for decorative print materials.

Often between the pages of an old book you will find a pressed flower because our ancestors saved blossoms for sentimental reasons. Today, prized flowers are not hidden in books but displayed under glass where their beauty can be enjoyed without fear of crumbling.

To understand the craftsmanship which is required to make a print of real flowers, a little study, thought and planning is necessary at the outset. The quality of a finished print is far more attractive if the natural color has been retained in plants and you will find that simplicity of design draws attention to the natural color and beauty of pressed flowers.

PLANT MATERIALS FOR PRINTS

There is always a question in the mind of the beginner as to what kind of plant materials to pick for use in a print. The thinner and lighter types of flowers, and other materials of similar quality, are the best ones with which to start. Pansies are one of the most satisfactory and Cosmos, Columbine, Petunias and Larkspur are also easy to process. Wild flowers, like Buttercup, Queen Anne's Lace and Goldenrod are also good beginning materials. The thicker types of flowers, like Tulips, Daffodils, Lilies or Geraniums, require more experienced handling because they must be split apart and reassembled in the design of a print. Not every type of flower can be pressed successfully but a list of some which have been tried is included at the end of this chapter.

All plant materials for a print are gathered when they have the least moisture, at noon on a sunny day. Flowers are picked at the height of their color peak which usually occurs just before a flower comes to full bloom. In selecting materials, choose those which are as perfect as possible.

The petals of a flower should be free of blemishes and any pollen should be gently brushed off, otherwise it will impair the color. It is advisable to press at least 2 extra pieces of each material because there is always a chance that a flower may have passed its color peak.

Plant stems for pressing need only be 5″ to 6″ long; in fact, an even shorter length is adequate. A thick stem, like that of a Tulip, is removed entirely. Foliage is cut from the stem, pressed separately and then put back later in the design.

PRESSING OF THE PLANT MATERIALS

Pressing is accomplished by inserting pieces of plant material between the folds of an absorbent paper. The surface of the paper must be extremely porous to withdraw the plant's moisture quickly and completely. Face tissues, paper towels or newspapers are adequate. The pages of an old telephone book are excellent for some pressing problems.

Five or 6 folds of paper must be used between each layer of plants. Plants should never touch one another while in process, or be placed closer than 1″ apart. In a square foot of paper, there is only enough absorbent quality to press a single layer of 3 or 4 pieces.

The manner in which the plants are placed between the folds of the paper determines the shape they will be and there can be no readjustment when the process is completed. The following examples are illustrative. Pansies are placed with their faces down on the paper, and their stems are bent to assure flatness. Wrinkles or folds in the petals

Robert Scharff

28. MAKING A FLOWER PRINT

These are the steps to follow and the equipment needed to make a flower print. On the left is the empty frame, next to it the pressed flowers partially arranged on the background and on the right, the finished print. At the bottom a selection of pressed flowers is shown together with scissors for cutting and tweezers for handling the flowers.

are carefully smoothed away. Daisies and Violets are pressed in a similar fashion. Petunias can be pressed full face, but if some are done in silhouette they add interest to a design. If Columbine is pressed in silhouette, it will display the spur on the flower.

When the plants have been carefully placed between the folds of the papers, and layers piled upon one another, an evenly distributed weight, such as a board or large book, is placed on top of the pile. This not only keeps the plant materials in contact with the absorbent paper but preserves their shapes.

To set color quickly and hasten removal of moisture, the papers are replaced with fresh ones after approximately 8 hours, and then again after an additional 8 hours. Thus, there are 3 complete sets of fresh papers used during the first 24 hours. The weight is replaced after changing papers. Replace the flower or leaf very carefully to retain its form. After the final change, materials remain for 2 to 3 weeks, to complete drying. If the plants are allowed to stay in the papers longer than necessary, the prolonged pressure impairs their color. Waxed paper or cellophane envelopes are adequate for storage until used.

It is fun to see how many types of materials can be pressed. Leaves, curling tendrils and graceful Ferns add variety to floral designs. Tiny Rose buds, like those which grow on the Polyantha, are wonderful to use for the edge of a design.

DESIGNING AND FRAMING PRINTS

Before you make your pressed materials into a design to go under glass, decide where you intend to hang it and what kind of a design is best suited. Your supply of plants will also be a factor.

You can use practically any idea and emphasize line, mass or grouped features in the motif. Designs with graceful rhythm in free flowing lines stress the naturalness of plants. Sometimes all lines may flow to one side of the print with a large Pansy or Tulip as a balancing center of interest. Other plants may be more adaptable to a design branching out from a central axis, like limbs on a tree. In another, the design may be a massed group, resembling a handful of flowers gathered in the garden.

Plants for print designs are used in natural color, not tinted or painted. Pressure holds the plants in the design position and no glue or paste is used. I tried an adhesive in several of my prints and it impaired the color of flowers in a couple of months, while those without it remained bright for years. A design will stay firmly in place when the pressure between the glass and the back of the frame is sufficient.

A background of some sort is required for a print and the mood and plant material of the print determine its nature. Backgrounds can be of paper or a textile. Soft colors and plain surfaces are more appropriate than vivid colors and patterned ones.

Drawing paper has a slightly rough surface which helps to hold materials in place and its creamy, soft tones are excellent. Elementary-school construction paper (the kind used for cutouts) has a plain surface and comes in delightful colors. Blotters, without a design, are another idea for a background.

Various fabrics are appropriate as backgrounds. Velvet not only brings out the color of pressed plants but also acts as a cushion to hold the design. Wool, cotton and linen fabrics are other good choices. Bright colored taffeta or silk makes an elegant background, but unfortunately its glossy surface hampers proper stabilization of the design. However, a thin, smooth layer of cotton (not over $\frac{1}{10}''$ to

⅛″ thick) can be used between this type of fabric and the back board of the frame, to supply enough pressure to hold materials in place.

There are two ways to assemble the design of pressed materials in a print. But no matter how it is done, it is a task which requires patience and perseverance.

In the first method, the background is firmly attached to the back board for the frame and the design made upon the face of it. A design is easier to establish if the key pieces are placed first, and the other items then worked into the proper position. Tweezers are an aid in maneuvering pieces since a trial and error method may be necessary to form the desired design. An illusion of depth can be attained by placing one piece upon another after clipping away any bulky areas.

When the design is completed the glass is placed upon it and the frame molding fitted around it. The three parts, design on the background, glass and frame, are turned over as a unit, with a quick, firm movement. As with any other picture the back is tacked in place and a gay piece of paper is glued on to the back for a finishing touch.

In the alternate method, the glass is left in the frame and the design of pressed materials made in reverse on it, instead of right side up on the background. If the proposed design is sketched beforehand, it lessens the chance of misplacing pieces. After completing the pattern, the background is placed on it and the back board tacked in the frame.

Each method is practical for making a print. The choice is up to you.

Stuart A. McQuade

29. VICTORIAN

Blue, lavender and purple predominate in this oval design in a gilt frame of pressed Pansies, Fuchsia, Clematis and individual florets of Delphinium. Fern tips, Sweet Pea vines and Mint leaves help soften and blend the design together.

Frames. The frame for a print is selected to fit the mood. Plain frames bring out the beauty of plants, while those of ornate character detract. Look around, there may be an old frame tucked away and long forgotten like one of the oval frames, so popular a century ago. Illustration 29 shows an oval design in such a frame. Silvered moldings are excellent for black velvet backgrounds, and white moldings are suitable for pastel colors. Modern plain wood frames have great possibilities.

USES FOR PRINTS

Every print of real flowers is an original worthy of an important place on the wall. A large print is suitable for a living room and an especially choice one could be the keynote of the entire decorative plan. Smaller, light-colored prints are charming on bedroom walls.

Prints may be hung singly, paired or grouped. In any group, frames and designs do not have to be identical if a feeling of similarity predominates. Anyone who loves flowers will enjoy using a group of her favorite prints on the wall. Hanging two or three prints of varying sizes is an interesting way to treat a long, bare wall space. Sometimes it is more decorative if one print is hung above another on a wide ribbon. If prints are hung on a patterned wall surface it is advisable to use a wide mat within the frame to give the design distinction.

HISTORICAL BACKGROUND OF FLOWER PRINTS

For over three hundred years, prints of flowers have been a popular form of art. Their origin can be traced to the botanist who used them as a means of recording his plants.

Such prints were the principal illustrations in English books of the sixteenth and seventeenth centuries and, as many of the early botanists were gifted artists, there exists a valuable record in old volumes. The English prints of the eighteenth century were superb in the perfection of detail and color. The creative genius of Robert J. Thornton produced some of the finest and "Temple of Flora," published about 1800, contained many of his best ones. His prints had elaborate detail in flowers and many were supplemented by scenic backgrounds indigenous to the natural habitat of the plant featured in the print.

George Ehret had a great influence on botanical illustrations because of the valuable record he left by dating and signing his works. Although he was German by birth, his major work was done in England during the eighteenth century. All his flower drawings show a marvelous technique and accuracy in every detail of flower construction.

Another outstanding name associated with English prints is that of Robert Furber. In 1730, he issued a commercial catalog called "Twelve Months of the Year" and copies of these famous large bouquet prints make beautiful decorations. A complete set of originals hangs on the stairwell of the George Wythe House in Colonial Williamsburg. Each flower in the set of twelve prints is arranged according to the month in which it bloomed, and each flower is numbered and named at the bottom.

In the United States, all early lithographers made flower prints. Some show flowers or fruits in all their dissected parts. Currier and Ives made numerous floral prints and they were typical of the Victorian taste. Many wonderful examples of American prints are to be found in old floral magazines, old botanies, nurserymen's magazines and horticultural journals. Godey's Lady's Book, the woman's magazine of yesterday, carried many prints in its issues. Today, with the great revival of interest in flower prints, a number of our household magazines are featuring them in their pages.

The nature of French prints is more decorative than scientific. Jean Louis Prevost and Pierre Joseph Redouté were masters and their style has never been equaled. The delicate color and perfection of detail are blended into designs of grace and elegance.

Old flower prints offer many inspirational ideas that can be worked into prints which are made of real flowers. The old print designs, whether English, French or American, will supply a basis for your own personal interpretation.

SUGGESTED IDEAS FOR PRINTS

The ideas for prints are legion and the following suggestions are offered to stimulate your imagination.

Bridal Prints.   Any bride loves to have a keepsake print which is made of the flowers from her bridal bouquet. This is a charming way to keep a few of the cherished blossoms

30. ROADSIDE BEAUTY

Ferns on a background of off-white drawing paper make the simple flowing design of this print framed in dark brown. In the lower portion the ferns were inverted to display their interesting under surfaces and to give a contrast in color.

Vincent Renna

for purely sentimental reasons. My first print of this kind was made for my daughter and since then many young brides have requested them. A small piece of the wedding gown can form the background and ribbons from the bouquet be used as part of the design. A white frame, with a touch of gold embellishment, supplies a perfect finishing touch. The illusion of an old-fashioned bouquet can be created by using the narrow edging of a lace paper doily to outline a round floral design. Another idea is to place the flowers in a complete circle suggesting a wedding ring.

Botanical Prints. There is something fascinating about a botanical print, when the design shows the form of the plant and its various stages of growth. Three spikes of Delphinium or Larkspur make a novel print if the spikes are pressed carefully. Fuchsia, shown in its stages from bud to full flower, is another interesting print idea. Other plants can be pressed to show their floral cycle in the print design.

Foliage Prints. Many kinds of leaves are suited to print designs. The only requirements are that the leaves be flat, colorful and interesting in form. Croton, for example, has fine leaves for this purpose.

Wild Materials Prints. Anyone with a love of the out-of-doors finds wild plants especially adaptable to charming designs. Grasses and wild flowers are always pleasing. The graceful shape of Ferns is emphasized under glass. (See

Illustration 30.) Often a soft blue is used for the background, to suggest the out-of-doors, and does a great deal to enrich the print.

Single Color Prints. Subtle, charming combinations can be made by choosing a single color for the print and using its various shades and tints in the design materials. Such designs are usually more effective on a neutral background.

For yellow use Acacia, Yellow Daisies, California Poppies and Daffodils. For blue prints use Delphinium, Cornflower, Pansy and other flowers in variations of blue. For an all-lavender print use Heather, Stock, Larkspur, Pansy, Petunia, Columbine and Violet.

Black Background Prints. Black backgrounds lend themselves to many striking combinations. Black velvet emphasizes the daintiness of Queen Anne's Lace, and Artemisia and white Cosmos are subtle combinations against black. Black makes skeletonized leaves appear more ghostlike.

Novelty Prints. People who collect Four-leaved Clovers can make them into interesting prints. Clovers formed into a horseshoe design on a neutral background with a black frame make an extremely decorative item for the wall.

Pressed Materials Under Glass Tops. Glass-covered furniture should not be overlooked as a conspicuous place to display pressed designs. Such designs are charming though they are not as lasting as when in a frame. When the surface is large several groupings, one larger than the other, work

Vincent Renna

out nicely. Under the glass of a vanity or dressing table is an excellent place to display designs of pale, dainty materials.

Miniatures. Miniature prints have many uses in the home. A single flower with its foliage is ample to fill a small frame. Small oval frames are charming with a few Violets or Pansies. There are endless ideas for making flower prints for your home.

31. SUMMER FLOWERS

A pair of prints using similar plant materials in opposite designs forms a single unit of decoration. The wood frame and cream background emphasize the colors in pink Larkspur, lavender Petunias and blue Delphinium while vine tendrils and leaves add a finishing touch.

CHART 6. SOME FLOWERS TO PRESS FOR PRINTS

This chart gives the names of flowers which have been pressed successfully. Other flowers with the same physical characteristics can be processed according to these suggestions.

NAME	SHAPE	PROCESSED	COLOR TO PRESS
ACACIA, *Acacia pubescens*	cluster	single cluster	yellow
AGERATUM, *Houstonianum*	tight heads	single head	blue, white
BABY GLADIOLUS, *Gladiolus tristis*	spike	single floret	white
BABY'S-BREATH, *Gypsophila*	small cups	stems	white
BEE BALM (Oswego Tea), *Monarda didyma*	tubular	single head	scarlet
BLEEDING HEART, *Dicentra spectabilis*	1-sided cluster	stem	rose
BUTTERFLY WEED, *Asclepias tuberosa*	loose cluster	cluster	orange
CANDYTUFT, *Iberis umbellata*	closed cluster	single cluster	all colors
CARNATION (Clove Pink), *Dianthus caryophyllus*	fr. petal head	singly	all colors
CLEMATIS (Virgin's-Bower), *Clematis jackmanii, C. montana*	circular	singly	white, purple, pink
COLUMBINE, *Aquilegia*	spurred	stem	red, pink, purple

Name	Form	Arrangement	Color
CORAL-BELLS (Alumroot), *Heuchera sanguinea*	tiny bells	stem	red
CORNFLOWER (Bachelor's-Button), *Centaurea cyanus*	tubular	singly	pink, blue
COSMOS, *Cosmos bipinnatus*	rayed	singly	white, pink, crimson
CROCUS, *Crocus vernus*	3-petaled tube	singly	all colors
DAFFODIL (Trumpet Narcissus), *Narcissus pseudo-narcissus*	long cup	singly	yellow
DELPHINIUM	single floret	singly	blue, violet
FORGET-ME-NOT, *Myosotis*	terminal racemes	stem	blue, pink
FREESIA	funnel	singly	yellow, lavender
FUCHSIA, *Fuchsia hybrida*	pendulous bells	singly	red, purple, white
GERANIUM (Storksbill), *Pelargonium*	umbell cluster	singly	red, pink
GLADIOLUS	spike	single floret	all colors
GOLDENROD, *Solidago*	cluster	single cluster	yellow
HEATHER, *Calluna*	spike	spike	purple
HELIOTROPE, *Heliotropium arborescens*	round cluster	cluster	pink, lavender
DAISY, PAINTED (Pyrethrum), *chrysanthemum coccineum*	rayed	singly	red, pink, white

SOME FLOWERS TO PRESS FOR PRINTS (*Cont.*)

Name	Shape	Processed	Color to Press
IRIS, Siberian or dwarf variety	6-petaled	singly	all colors
JONQUIL, *Narcissus jonquilla*	cluster	singly	yellow
LARKSPUR, *Delphinium ajacis*, annual garden variety	spike	spike	blue, pink, lavender
LILAC, *Syringa vulgaris*	cluster	cluster	lavender
LILY OF THE VALLEY, *Convallaria majalis*	bell	stem	white
MARIGOLD, FRENCH, *Tagetes patula*	rayed	singly	red to yellow
MORNING-GLORY, *Ipomoea pandurata*	round	singly	purple, pink, blue
NARCISSUS, *Narcissus poeticus*	ring-shaped cup	singly	yellow
NASTURTIUM, *Tropaeolum majus*	5-petaled	singly	yellow, orange, red
PANSY (Heartsease), *Viola tricolor hortensis*	5-petaled	singly	blue, yellow
POPPY, CALIFORNIA, *Eschscholtzia californica*	4-petaled	singly	yellow
PRIMROSE, *Primula*	umbell	singly	red, blue, yellow

Name	Cluster	Arrangement	Colors
QUEEN ANNE'S LACE (Wild Carrot), *Daucus carota*	umbell	singly	white
ROSE, polyantha variety	many-petaled	singly	red, pink, yellow
SALVIA (Garden Sage), *Salvia officinalis*	spike	spike	purple
(Scarlet Sage), *Salvia splendens*	spike	spike	scarlet
SEA LAVENDER, *Limonium*	branched spike	spike	lavender, rose, blue
SNAPDRAGON (Toad's-Mouth), *Antirrhinum*	spike	single flower	rose, red, yellow
SQUILL (Bluebell), *Scilla*	bell	singly	blue, purple
STATICE (Sea Pink) or (Thrift)	small	stem	all colors
SWEET PEA, *Lathyrus latifolius*, perennial variety	many-petaled	singly	crimson
Lathyrus odoratus, annual variety	"	"	all colors
SWEET WILLIAM (Bush Pink), *Dianthus barbatus*	dense cluster	singly	rose, purple
TULIP, *Tulipa*, cottage, early, parrot varieties	bell	singly	red, yellow, pink
VERBENA, *Verbena hortensis*	compact cluster	singly	pink, red, yellow
VIOLET, *Viola odorata*	5-petaled	singly	violet, white
WILD BERGAMOT, *Monarda fistulosa*	globular	single head	blue
ZINNIA, *Zinnia*, Mexican lilliput varieties	cone head	singly	all colors

CHART 7. SOME FOLIAGES TO PRESS FOR PRINTS

This chart gives the names of foliages which have been pressed successfully. Other foliages with the same physical characteristics can be processed according to these suggestions.

NAME	SHAPE	PROCESSED	COLOR WHEN DRIED
ACACIA, *Acacia pubescens*	fine, feathery	stem	silvery green
ARTEMISIA (Wormwood), *Artemisia albula*	felty, lobed	stem	gray
BEE BALM (Oswego Tea), *Monarda didyma*	pointed oval	singly	green
BEECH, EUROPEAN, *Fagus sylvatica*	lobed, ovate	stem, singly	green
CAT'S-EAR, *Hypochaeris radicata*	oval	singly	gray
CLOVER, *Trifolium*	compounded	singly	gray-green
COLUMBINE, *Aquilegia*	compounded	singly	light green
CROTON, *Codiaeum*	small sizes	singly	light colors
DUSTY MILLER (Wormwood), *Artemisia stelleriana*	small, toothed	singly	white
FUCHSIA, *Fuchsia hybrida*	oval, lance	singly	gray-green
GALAX, *Galax aphylla*	heart	singly	green, brown
GERANIUM (Storksbill), *Pelargonium*	roundish, lobed	singly	gray-green

Plant	Leaf	Arrangement	Color
IVY, ENGLISH, *Hedera helix*	3-5-lobed	singly	green
MAPLE, JAPANESE, *Acer palmatum*	lobed, divided	branch	scarlet
MINT (Spearmint), *Mentha spicata*	marginal toothed	stem	green
MULLEIN, *Verbascum thapsus*	wooly, oblong	singly	gray
PANSY (Heartsease), *Viola tricolor hortensis*	heart	singly	green
PLANTAIN LILY, *Hosta*	small sizes	singly	green, tan
POPPY, CALIFORNIA, *Eschscholtzia californica*	fine, feathery	singly	light green
SWEET PEA, PERENNIAL, *Lathyrus latifolius*	linear	singly	light green
VIOLET, *Viola odorata*	heart	singly	dark green
WOOLY LAMB'S-EAR, *Stachys lanata*	wooly, oval	singly	white

14. Plaques

Plaques are a comparatively new and unusual idea for a wall decoration. They consist of a design made with dried plants permanently mounted on a firm background. Since the long narrow shape is prevalent, they are often referred to as panels. Here is a whole new field for the homemaker to explore.

Any home decorator who is looking for something different will find that plaques are individual enough to call attention to any wall on which they are hung. Ideas for design are so varied that there is one to suit every decorative need. Their effectiveness is only fully realized when a plaque is made and hung on the wall.

The large display of plaques, by the Garden Club of America at the New York International Flower Show several years ago, contributed much to their wide popularity. These plaques included fascinating designs of plants with interesting forms, pleasing colors and a variety of textures. They attracted crowds to the exhibit and many of the spectators were stimulated to make a plaque themselves. A plaque is fun to make and anyone can do it, for training or expert skill is not required.

MAKING A PLAQUE

An unframed piece of wood is the generally accepted surface upon which to mount the design of dried plants. A thin type of wood, like plywood, is a good surface to begin with. A piece approximately 10″ by 20″ is easy to handle and its design requires only a small quantity of plant materials. The wood may be any shape—square, round, oval, oblong or rectangular. Raw or new wood should have some kind of finish applied to it before the design is mounted. Methods of applying simple finishes are given at the end of this chapter.

All the plants should be thoroughly dried before they are placed in the design. From the various drying techniques described in previous chapters choose the one which will give the result you wish. In general, plants are used in a natural state but there may be instances when artificial treatment, like varnishing or gilding, is required for a special effect.

What kind of plants shall you use? A variety of types and kinds will contribute to an interesting design. Seed pods, nuts, cones and leaves are popular. A curling tendril or a twig has a graceful sweeping line which may be used in a design. Grasses, dried fruits, gourds and fungus are other possibilities. A more complete listing of materials suitable for designs appears at the end of the chapter.

The plant pieces may have to be tried in numerous positions before a satisfactory design is achieved. I find it is helpful to cut a piece of heavy paper or cardboard the same size as the background and use this for working out the various parts in the design. It prevents scratching or marring the finish on the wood and when the design is ready for permanent mounting, the pieces can be transferred in one operation.

Even if a person is talented enough to work freehand, a light tracery of dots on the wood helps to indicate the proper position for key pieces. Such small dots are easily covered. The work of designing should be done carefully and slowly. A good design does require time but remember it will be a lasting decoration.

The favored technique is to attach the plants to the background with a colorless plastic adhesive, but I prefer to use clear glue. Toothpicks, used as applicators, avoid soiling both hands and plants. A small quantity of the adhesive is spread on the back of one piece at a time. Each piece is pressed firmly into position and held there for several seconds. After all the pieces of a design have been glued in place the plaque is laid flat and left undisturbed for 24 hours until the glue is firmly hardened.

Any idea may be used to organize the plants provided it adheres to the established design principles of proportion, balance, rhythm and interest. The relationship of the design's elements to the dimensions of the background surface is an important factor. When the plants are restricted to a half to a third of the entire area of the wood, the expanse of unornamented surface gives a feeling of spacious-

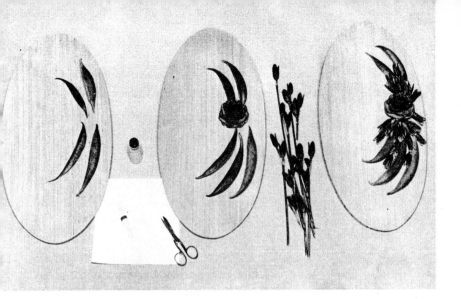

Robert Scharff

32. MAKING A PLAQUE

A plaque is shown here in three stages of its development to the finished product on the right. The equipment needed is arranged on the left: a bottle of clear glue with toothpicks for applying it to the dried plants and a pair of scissors for cutting.

ness. A finely finished piece of wood is far more dramatic with a small quantity of plants but another type of background may need a fuller design. Personality and good taste are the guides.

The success of any design depends on the manner in which form, color and texture of the plants are used. Plaques have an outstanding character when one or more of these elements is emphasized.

Variety in shape, size and outline of plants is necessary for an interesting design. One way to achieve interest is to place some of the design pieces flat, and others in silhouette. Long spikes placed in silhouette may be balanced by round forms. Another way to introduce variety is to use some pods with seeds and others without. Still another way is to split seed pods and place some with the exterior and others with the interior surface visible.

Color may be used to emphasize a design. Light colors in plants can be complemented by those of darker tones. Pods which have colored seeds or color in their linings and cones with color splashes on their scales add interesting variations. Contrast in color values between pieces of a design and the background is one way to establish interest. Repetition of color will give rhythm and balance. Color in plaques is as important as in any other artistic design.

The quality of a plant surface determines its texture, or it may be better defined by saying it is the way the plant feels to the touch. Dried plants have many textures but smooth, rough and prickly are the most common. An interplay of these textures gives distinction to a plaque design.

SOURCES OF IDEAS FOR PLAQUES

Where can you find an idea for a plaque design? There is much interesting material written on the subject of design that is helpful in the quest for ideas. A working acquaintance with historical designs is a fruitful source of ideas. If you live near a museum a visit there will provide ample inspiration. It is neither desirable nor necessary to try to copy the elaborate details in historical design but an intelligent application of an idea makes an excellent start for plaque design.

The swag, basket and garland designs which are seen so frequently today are copied from the works of the great carver of three hundred years ago, Grinling Gibbons. As a master of wood carving he had a marvelous technique for executing every detail of fruits, vegetables and flowers. There are many pieces of dried plants which have the character and feeling of wood and so can be adapted to a design which resembles a carving.

BACKROUNDS FOR PLAQUES

Many kinds of wood are adequate backgrounds for a plaque. Modern methods of production emphasize grain and texture of the wood itself and varieties of light and dark tones are available wherever wood is sold. Some woods are raw and they need finishing, while others are ready for use. A neighborhood lumberyard will tailor wood to required size and shape.

Many old or used pieces of wood have great possibilities for the backgrounds of plaques. Two old cypress shingles provided wonderful mounting surfaces for a pair of long narrow plaques. Years of exposure to the elements brought out the natural wood grain and produced a finish which would be hard to duplicate. The mellow tone of these shingles formed an excellent foil for a design of dried plants.

Art stores have materials which can be substituted for wood such as illustration, mat or canvas board. I have used

heavy illustration board as a background for a number of my plaques and it is quite effective. Such surfaces are easy to cut to any desired shape and need not be painted unless you so desire.

A design of dried plants is distinctive when it is executed on an old willow or rattan tray. Either of these is an excellent background for a semicircular or circular pattern. If a length of fairly wide ribbon is used as a means of attaching the tray to the wall, it turns out to be an unusual plaque.

The mats which are in the stores today for use on dining tables are satisfactory for plaque backgrounds. Those which are made of straw fiber, split bamboo or heavy thread are the most suitable. (See Illustration 33.) Sometimes with a mat of heavy thread or straw, the plants may be sewn on with a darning needle and heavy thread. Each piece is attached to the background with one or two loops of the thread hidden in some part of the plant's form. For example, in using a spike of Mullein, dark thread can be cleverly concealed between the small seed cases on the long stalk. This is an easy and simple way to make a plaque but limited in the variety of plants or kinds of designs you can use.

33. DESIGN TO LIVE WITH

In decided contrast to the bamboo mat is this grouped design of cut cones, Buckeyes and small Coconuts with seed pods from Siberian Iris, Senna, Lily and Yucca fanning out at the top and bottom.

incent Renna

THE USE OF COLOR IN PLAQUES

Color is indispensable in home furnishings and almost any color can be used for the background of a plaque if the dried plants are chosen to blend with it. To key the color of a background to the setting of a room is an unusual and interesting device. Shades of mellon, coral, green or turquoise will create a dramatic effect. Brown cones or seed pods are impressive against dusty rose or chartreuse backgrounds. Green and gray plants can produce distinctive plaques if they are used with white or light-colored backgrounds.

The values of brown predominate in plaques since wood is universally considered an appropriate background. There are lovely shades of brown, from beige to rich chocolate. There is a wide choice in size and shape since so many plants turn brown when they are dried.

Gray has a serene character which is adaptable to many plaque ideas. Its neutral color may be warm or cool and ranges in value from light tints to deep charcoal. Though to many people gray does not have the same emotional appeal as other colors, you will discover that gray-toned plants combine into subtle, fascinating monotone plaques. A monotone plaque is one in which the design of dried plants and the background are limited to one color with a wide difference in value.

FRAMES FOR PLAQUES

The majority of plaques are unframed but sometimes the addition of a frame enhances their artistic value. Plain wood frames may be used on nearly all types of plaques.

Old frames, whose finish has mellowed in tone with the years, are suited to some designs while simple modern frames make others look like a million dollars.

A frame for a plaque should repeat some of the feeling of the design materials. When the background of the plaque is light and the plants have a dainty quality, a narrow light-colored molding is appropriate. On the other hand a frame which is made of bamboo requires plants of a sturdier nature, like seed pods, nuts, cones or branches.

USES FOR PLAQUES

A plaque should be related to the furnishings in a room. Plaques can be planned to harmonize with any décor. In a formal room nothing is more suitable than a rich dark-wood plaque with a compatible design of dried plants. In an Early American setting, the design might be a casual grouping of native materials on a piece of pine or maple. The plaque for a modern room would emphasize the form of the plants in a streamlined pattern on a piece of wood with a modern finish.

Single pictures or prints on the walls of our homes are now being replaced by mass groupings. These groups include not only pictures of every description but other types of decorative objects—anything from plates to miniatures. Plaques can be included in such groups to supply unusual interest and variety.

A plaque should be placed where it is seen to the best advantage. A long narrow one with a horizontal design is extremely effective when hung over a mantel. In fact the result can resemble a wood carving. For such a plaque select a piece of hard wood, about 20″ by 40″. Give it a rich mellow finish and bevel the edge. The flowing lines of a garland or festoon are an excellent design idea. The dried plants should be selected in somewhat the same color value but differing in size, form and texture. A raised or carved effect is achieved by securing one piece of plant material in its place and allowing the adhesive to harden before another is placed near or upon it. The raised design may be built up an inch or more. The larger pieces of plant materials, like cones or pods, may have enough natural thickness to provide the desired depth. (See Illustration 35.)

Two pieces of wood which are exactly alike in shape and size can be used as backgrounds for a pair of plaques. If all the lines in the design of one plaque are swung to the right and those in the other to the left, and they are hung facing one another, they will form a balanced unit.

Before concluding my discussion of plaques I want to stress that the same technique of attaching dried plants to wood may be used to decorate the frames of pictures or mirrors. They can be ornamented in many styles and adapted to any room. All you need is a box of dried plants, a little imagination and the will to be a bit daring.

Recently an antique frame came into my possession and wishing to give it some degree of distinction I gathered together woody-textured pieces like cones, nuts, acorns and

34. CASUAL CHARM

This plaque was fashioned from materials gathered by the roadside—grasses, grains, Acorns, Hemlock and burrs—and informally grouped on a piece of plywood.

Robert Schar

35. WOOD CARVING

This design is mounted on a Walnut panel and uses Pine, Douglas Fir and Redwood cones along with a variety of seed pods from Mullein, Okra, Columbine, Butterfly Weed and the Eucalyptus tree. For added interest Acorns, nuts and panicles of Sea Oat are placed through the design.

seed pods. I massed these in wreath fashion keeping the outline narrow and pieces close together. The frame and dried plants are well suited to one another and the result is an unusual and extremely lovely combination. Any inexpensive picture frame could be decorated in the same way.

Many offices have wood paneling on the walls and the textures and forms of dried plants on plaques are highly appropriate. One type of plaque would serve as a point of conversation in a waiting or conference room or another would add a modern touch in a lobby or showroom.

FINISHES FOR PLAQUES

All raw wood for backgrounds should be aged, clean and free of marks or blemishes. Any cutting, beveling or smoothing of the wood is done before the finish is applied. The following are easy ways to finish a piece of wood for the background of a plaque. Books, magazines or the local paint store have adequate directions for special finishes.

Wax. With a pad of soft dampened cloth apply a thin coat of paste wax to the wood. Rub the wax into the wood and allow to dry, then polish before another coat is applied. Two applications make a good finish.

Shellac. With a brush apply a coat of shellac to the wood. Allow the shellac to dry before another coat is applied. Use very fine sandpaper lightly between coats of shellac for a smooth finish. Two or three coats of shellac are ample for a satisfactory finish.

Varnish. Like shellac, varnish is applied with a brush and allowed to dry between coats. Varnish may appear to dry quickly yet it remains tacky a long time. Sandpaper as with shellac. Several thin coats of varnish are better than one heavy one.

Tinting. The various colors of paint from tubes such as artists use achieve striking results. Dilute the paint with turpentine until the consistency of cream, and rub into the wood with a small pad of cloth. When the paint is dry, a coat of wax makes the finish permanent.

CHART 8. SEED PODS AND OTHER MATERIALS FOR PLAQUES

SEED PODS

CLUSTER

AGAVE
ALDER, BLACK, *Alnus vulgaris*
MAGNOLIA, *Magnolia grandiflora*
MALLOW, *Malva*
PAULOWNIA

RED GUM, *Eucalyptus rostrata*
TORNILLO, *Strombocarpa odorata*
TRAVELER'S-TREE, *Ravenala madagascar-iensis*

ROUND

CHINESE LANTERN PLANT, *Physalis alke-kengi*
GLOBE THISTLE, *Echinops*

SWEET GUM, *Liquidambar*
SYCAMORE, *Platanus occidentalis*

CONE-SHAPED

LOTUS, *Nelumbium*
POPPY, ORIENTAL, *Papaver orientale*

SNEEZEWEED, *Helenium*
STERCULIA

LONG

ACACIA
CATALPA, *Catalpa bignonioides*
LOCUST, *Robinia*

SENNA, *Cassia*
SWEET PEA, *Lathyrus latifolius*
TRUMPET VINE, *Campsis radicans*

OKRA, *Hibiscus esculentus*
POINCIANA, ROYAL, *Delonix regia*

WISTERIA
WOMAN'S-TONGUE TREE, *Albizzia lebbek*

SPIKE

BOTTLE BRUSH, *Callistemon*
CATTAIL (Reed), *Typha*
PLANTAIN LILY, *Hosta*

MOTH MULLEIN, *Verbascum blattaria*
MULLEIN, *Verbascum thapsus*

PRICKLY TEXTURE

CASTOR BEAN, *Ricinus communis*
GLOBE THISTLE, *Echinops*

SWEET GUM, *Liquidambar*
TEASEL, *Dipsacus*

SPRAY

FALSE OR WILD INDIGO, *Baptisia*
COLUMBINE, *Aquilegia*
GAS PLANT, *Dictamnus albus*
DOCK, *Rumex*

EUCALYPTUS (Gum Tree)
MILKWEED, *Asclepias*
YUCCA

FLOWER FORM

PEONY, *Paeonia*

WOOD ROSES, *Ipomoea tuberosa*

OVAL

IRIS, SIBERIAN, *Iris sibirica*
LILY

TULIP, *Tulipa*

SEED PODS AND OTHER MATERIALS FOR PLAQUES (*Cont.*)

NUTS

ACORN   HICKORY
ALMOND   PEANUT
BLACK WALNUT   PECAN
BRAZIL   WALNUT
CHESTNUT

OTHER MATERIALS

BERRIES   GRASSES
BURRS   GRAINS
COCONUT CALYX   GOURDS
CONES, all kinds   LEAVES
DRIED FRUITS   SEEDS
DATE SPRAYS, Palm TWIGS
FUNGUS   TENDRILS, vine

15. Painting Dried Plants

Painting dried plants is fun and a challenge to anyone with imagination and a flair with a paint brush. If you try your hand at it you will be rewarded by the enthusiastic admiration of some friends and amused by the vigorous denunciation of others. Either way, the painted materials become a conversation piece.

Painted plants are highly adaptable to the home and a phase of flower arrangement which could well become more popular among women who enjoy using color and plants for home decoration. The lasting quality is one of their greatest assets. During the winter months when fresh materials are limited, it is satisfying and economical to use plants you have dried and painted. Every housekeeper has her "blue days" and applying color to dried plants may provide just the lift she needs.

In painting plants, natural color should be emphasized. Avoid such unreal effects as pink leaves and blue branches or blue-and-white-striped seed pods!

A great majority of dried plants have naturally lovely color and do not require painting. Paint gives a new lease on life, however, to plants in good physical condition but whose color is unattractive. Some dried plants, like gourds or seed pods, are sturdy enough to withstand several paintings. Tropical plants have this quality and some of my Coconut Calyxes have changed color several times.

All plants should be thoroughly dry and free of dust or loose particles before paint is applied. As in any painting, a clean surface is required for good adhesion.

KINDS OF PAINT

Various kinds of paint are appropriate for coloring dried plants and as each one produces a different result, the choice is made according to the effect desired.

Enamel. Quick-dry enamel, the commonest type of paint on the market, can be purchased in a wide range of colors. It is simple to apply and one coat usually is sufficient. Two coats may be necessary to transform a dark piece to a lighter shade.

Interior Paint. Water soluble, casein, rubber-base or flat paints, popular for interior finishes, can be used on dried plants. If you have some left after painting walls or ceilings, why not use it for this. One winter, all my decorations were dominated by white branches due to excess ceiling paint! The chief advantage of rubber-base paints is that once a plant is colored, it may be washed without much loss of color.

Poster Paint. Poster paint is the easiest of all to use on dried plants. Any amateur can do a job that looks professional. It dries within an hour and produces a dull soft finish more appropriate than the high gloss of enamel. Poster paint should be applied with a brush. The art stores carry it in a wide range of colors in small, inexpensive jars. Since it is a water mix, it may be readily removed. Watercolor paints may be substituted but their transparent quality makes it a little more difficult to obtain deep colors.

Tube Paint. Artist's tube colors are excellent and any effect is possible with this type of paint. You do not require a paint box with all its fittings; all you need are four tubes of paint, red, blue, yellow and white; one or two small brushes and a little turpentine. The tube paint is too thick without dilutions, so add a little turpentine until it spreads easily on the plants. A piece of aluminum foil, or an old pie tin, is quite adequate for mixing the paint. If you have not used tube-type paint or feel a little unsure of yourself, spend half an hour mixing small quantities and daubing to see the results. You will be amazed at the variations. Tube colors dry slowly and it may be as long as a week before you can use the plants. This depends upon weather, thickness of paint and the amount of turpentine.

WAYS TO APPLY PAINT

By Brush. Use a small camel's-hair brush to apply the type of paint you choose. All the paints I've mentioned can be applied with a brush.

By Dipping.   Pour paint into a container large enough to submerge the plant and apply paint by dipping the plant into the container. This method is excellent for materials like cones or seed pods with many openings that would be difficult to cover with a brush.

By Spraying.   A variety of paints are available in spray cans. Pressure on the nozzle applies paint to dried plants quickly and easily. Paint can also be applied with a vacuum-cleaner sprayer, but a little practice is necessary to produce an even coating.

IDEAS FOR COLORING DRIED PLANTS

Chalk crayons (pastels) are easily applied and produce surprising results on dried plants. Their delicate pastel colors are wonderful for light or dainty materials. Pastels have only one disadvantage: they wear off, unless covered by a transparent fixative.

A large cone can be transformed into several attractive flowers, by cutting the center stem of scales into thin discs, then painting the individual scales in each disc to look like the petals of a flower. By following the natural color gradation pattern on petals, lighter at the outer edge and deepening to the center, the disc becomes a flower. A little white on the outer edge adds a finishing touch. Foliage painted with a similar grading of colors is striking.

A simple way to be sure of a pleasing combination is to paint the container and the plants to correspond with each other. Naturally the shape and color of the chosen container will determine the plants, their color, and the design you use.

Interesting compositions can be developed with a chartreuse container. Its yellow-green color suggests that either yellow or green would be a harmonious choice for the design plants. Using yellow for the theme, start by selecting and painting branches in a light value of yellow, for the height and outline of the design; next, select 6 seed pods of varying sizes and shapes for the transitional materials, and paint them in a deeper yellow; then choose a large form or a group of smaller ones, to be placed near the rim of the container, and for accent paint these orange. Lastly, select and paint 6 or 8 medium-sized yellow leaves, possibly outlining the veins in a dark color, and place them throughout the design for interest.

This basic pattern of using harmonious color relationship of plants and container can be carried out in any color. If you like to contrast colors but they seem to clash, use gray, tan or brown plants, to make the transition less obvious.

There is no reason why you cannot mix painted with naturally dried plants. An arrangement in a copper container of large dried brown leaves and seed pods or cones, painted in mellon or peach color, is effective. Many leaves, such as Lemon (Shallon), remain green and combining them with creamy-white painted plants is refreshing and different.

If you like to give your imagination free reign and are a bit daring, try a black-and-white combination. For example, painted white branches and leaves with natural black Baptisia pods and Teasel, in a black or white container is smartly modern. Every home cannot use this dramatic type of decoration but in several modern interiors I know it would be stunning.

Today the application of color to dried plants by chemicals or dye is done on a large scale and commercially colored plants are plentiful in gift shops, department stores and florist displays. The coloring is usually so bizarre that it cannot escape the eye of the shopper. Any devotee of natural color in plants shudders at the harsh artificial hues, and wonders how a person with any artistic sense could try to make them into satisfying designs.

Formerly, the use of artificially colored plants was frowned upon but now that our attitude has become more liberal toward decorative materials, painted plants are used in fascinating and unusual ways for home decorations. Plants should be painted with imagination and a discriminating selection of color. Never should they be a hodgepodge of intense hues but rather soft harmonious colors emphasizing naturalness.

16. Holiday Decorations

An eventful month starts at Thanksgiving and culminates in the celebration of Christmas. Any good hostess realizes that a well-decorated house adds to the festivities and the holiday spirit can start at the front door and carry through the entire house, even to the kitchen.

First, plan to use plants which are easy and inexpensive to obtain. Some people may enjoy sending to faraway places for exotic plants but it will put less strain on your time and budget to use those which you have collected locally.

Second, be practical by using dried plants to eliminate the necessity of frequent change. Such decorations will be as attractive at New Year's as they were before Christmas and will possibly last for another holiday season.

Whether you prefer restrained or elaborate decorations, you will find a collection of dried plants indispensable in creating effective designs for doors, mantel or table. Since this is the busiest season of the year, what a tremendous help it can be if you have prepared plants at a time of leisure and thus avoided a great deal of the last-minute rush.

THANKSGIVING

Thanksgiving is typically an American celebration and each year we are linked to our Pilgrim ancestors by carrying out customs bequeathed to us by them. Corn and Pumpkin were a part of the first Thanksgiving and are still used to express our thanks for the bounty of harvest.

Tying 3 ears of Corn by their husks to the front door is a popular traditional custom to signify to all who pass the hospitality in your home. Yours can be the gayest and most individual door on the street by adding other dried plants to the Corn to make a swag.

As the base of a swag use 1 or 2 long pieces of dried plants, such as a seed spike of Mullein or Yucca, sturdy enough to stand the strain of having other pieces tied to it. Place all the plants in a swag so that they hang downwards—30″ to 40″ is an adequate length for an average door. The first basic pieces may be put together on a flat surface but it is advisable to construct the major portion of a swag in a hanging position, balancing one part against the weight of another. Various kinds of dried plants, like grasses, grains, corn, leaves, nuts, cones or seed pods, may be used. Even artificial fruits are feasible since they are so beautifully made today. Several wrappings of string are enough to hold the design in place if tightly bound and securely knotted. A loop of the string is left on the reverse side of the swag, about a third of the way down, as a means of attachment. The husks of the Corn are excellent to cover the string for when they are dampened they may be bent to almost any shape.

There are many ways to vary a swag and you will enjoy thinking of different combinations. They are not limited to the front door but can be placed in other parts of the house. One may be hung at either or both ends of a mantel, beside a long upright mirror or in the long narrow space between 2 windows. A swag gives the feeling of an old-fashioned, rural Thanksgiving to a home not situated in the country. Illustration 36 shows a swag which was made in the manner described.

Living Room. Thanksgiving decorations for the living room will vary with the furnishings. In some homes a bowl of Gourds and Corn is effective while in others a large sheaf of bleached Barley accented by fresh fruits is more suitable. (Fruits, incidentally, need not be restricted to use in the dining room.) Chrysanthemums are glorious at this season with both bright and dark colors to select from. Stunning combinations can be made with 2 or 3 large Chinese or Spider Chrysanthemums and dried foliage. The Pompon varieties look better with dried branches.

Arrangements in copper or brass containers add a bright note to the decorations. Also a large metal tray makes an excellent background for arrangements. Dried plants in autumn colors form a charming composition with the glint of metal.

Small arrangements on end or coffee tables add to the

over-all picture. There are many ways to work brightly colored dried plants into small containers which may be as varied as the tables upon which they stand. The brilliant Bittersweet berry is adaptable to such containers, as are a number of grasses, seed pods, Strawflowers or Goldenrod. Any design may be supplemented by fresh plants.

Dining Room. Today a decoration is as necessary as the turkey on the Thanksgiving dinner table. A bowl of fruit has been the traditional Thanksgiving table decoration but this year why not try another idea to demonstrate your skill as an arranger. The cornucopia or horn of plenty, while not new, is appropriate for a table piece. This design is not limited to a cornucopia container but may also be worked out with a bowl or dish set on edge or even with an old scoop or a hat. The hat idea was described in Chapter 14, and the same principle can be carried out with other containers.

The bounty of harvest can be expressed in many ways but the idea you choose should harmonize with the dining table and its appointments of linen, china and glassware. You can use a well-finished board or an attractively shaped tray or mirror as a stand and construct a design directly upon it. A candle mold, a wooden bowl or an unusual basket have wonderful possibilities. For containers, a series

36. FALL SWAG

Mullein forms the background for this grouping suggestive of the harvest season with grasses and grains at the top and a variety of seed pods from Milkweed, Trumpet Vine, Sweet Gum and Teasel tapering down to the bottom.

Robert Scharff

of small pumpkins, graduated in size, are suitable for holding dried plants. If you prefer to use only fruits for a design, the addition of a dark note with cones, nuts or seed pods will emphasize their forms and quality.

Grain is highly suggestive of Thanksgiving and you are not limited to Wheat because Oats, Barley, Rye or Millet are also obtainable. When you are pressed for time, try one of my favorite ways to create an easy, effective table piece. Use a branched candelabrum and tie a sweeping bunch of grain to the base at either side, with a narrow ribbon of a neutral color. The sweep may be vertical or horizontal, depending on the table space. Finish by adding several lush bunches of grapes near the ribbons. The light color of grain is effective with a gold candelabrum, green candles and green grapes while black and green grapes are stunning with a silver one.

As place cards, leaves are charming, unusual and practical. You may gather large perfect leaves at any time and dry them in a flat form as described in Method #1 in Chapter 7. Many kinds of leaves are appropriate but Oak leaves with their interesting silhouette pattern are among the best. The leaf is used lengthwise and the name of each guest can be written on it with white ink.

Corsages. Providing corsages for your Thanksgiving guests is a gracious gesture. A few pieces of dried plants can be fashioned into a delightful corsage that costs practically nothing but a little imagination and the time it takes to construct it. Small corsages, 6″ to 7″ long, are made either by using 1 basic piece and adding others for em-

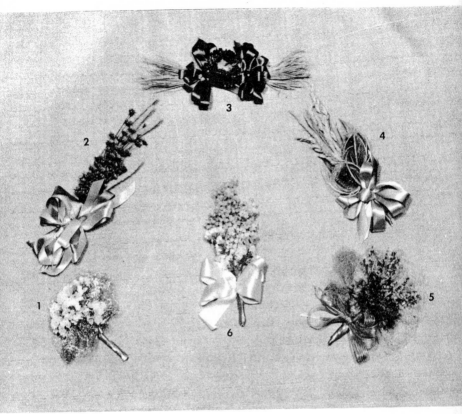

37. CORSAGES

1. White Statice with silver metallic lace   2. Tan grasses and tiny pink Strawflowers with a pink bow   3. Red-brown grasses and red Strawflowers with red ribbon 4. Green grass and Teasel with a green bow   5. Lavender and white Statice with a variegated ribbon bow and a frill of starched lavender lace   6. Yellow Acacia and Statice with a yellow bow.

phasis or by grouping small pieces into a cluster. For ease in wearing, they should be kept as light as possible by clipping away all unnecessary parts. There are only 2 essential points to watch: wire securely, and tape firmly. Fine threadlike wire is fastened to each piece before it is placed in the design and several turns of wire are added to hold all of the pieces together. For neatness, use florist corsage tape (parafilm) which sticks to itself and forms a skinlike covering for both stems and wire. To each corsage add a small, suitably colored ribbon bow as a perky finishing touch.

The following are some of my favorite ideas for corsages:

Hemlock Cones make an interesting corsage and 8 to 12 will be required for a design. Each cone is wired separately before it is put into the design. If they are fairly evenly matched, the result will be better.

Unusual flowerlike corsages can be made with Milkweed Pods, dried without their silky tufts, with a few bright berries inserted in each pod. Many other kinds of smaller seed pods are appropriate for corsages and shellacking or varnishing the finished corsage gives them a luster and improves their lasting quality.

Any of the pastel Statices are useful for dainty combinations. I use a frill of starched lace (available at the florist's in different colors) and 2 blending colors of Statice, as in Illustration 37.

Wheat or Grasses and 1 or 2 Strawflowers form a charming combination.

Kitchen. Even with all our modern timesaving methods and appliances, a homemaker must spend many hours in her kitchen and, like the rest of the home, this work center should be cheerfully decorated. An ordinary vegetable like Squash or Eggplant can be turned into a container by hollowing out a small portion and inserting decorative materials like Grass, Corn tassel, berries and autumn leaves. A wooden salad bowl or a tray is charming with gaily colored ears of Corn. You will find that an Italian wine bottle looks well with Wheat and red Onions or Grapes. Try filling a French lettuce basket with Gourds and Squash for a lively arrangement. Onion soup casseroles or small jelly molds are excellent as window-sill containers and the color and style of your kitchen will determine the materials you choose for them.

CHRISTMAS

At Christmas, Christian people all over the world unite in celebrating the Christ Child's birthday. No matter where you live, north, east, south or west, the gaily decorated homes, churches and shops are a joy to behold. It would be hard to imagine this day devoid of all its life, color and pageantry.

This is the time of year everyone becomes a decorator and strives to adorn the home to reflect the happiness of the festive season. In trimming your house for the holidays, you are not restricted by rules but are at liberty to decorate anything in any way you choose. Since the beliefs of many lands are blended in our population, each family has its own customs, traditions and decorating ideas. There are various schools of thought about Christmas decorations, and whether you favor natural, traditional decorations or the glitter and sparkle of artificial ones, dried plants can form the mainstay of satisfying and lasting decorative pieces.

Cones.   In decorating for Christmas, there is no substitute for cones. With their great versatility they fit into many design ideas and are equally attractive whether left natural or artificially colored. You may collect, dry and make cones into decorations at any time of year. Summer is a wonderful time to make a Christmas wreath of cones.

Since the days of the Renaissance, a wreath has been a symbolic Christmas motif and a cone wreath is a thing of beauty. Here's the way to make one:

A circular shape of wire, twigs or plywood is necessary as a base upon which to anchor the cones. Wire rings are far superior to bent coat hangers and they may be purchased from a florist in varying sizes. One of 16″ diameter allows enough room to work comfortably and makes an attractive decoration.

To prevent the materials from slipping, the ring should be wrapped with narrow strips of material. The rubbery surface of corsage tape is excellent because it sticks to itself, making the winding easier. The first end is attached with a piece of Scotch Tape and the corsage tape tossed over and over until the circle is covered. Another piece of Scotch Tape fastens the end of the circle.

A length of either wire or florist string is attached to

38. GOLDEN CONES

Cones of various sizes, some cut into sections and others inverted, are fastened to a pasteboard circle with heads of Teasel added for contrast and the whole sprayed with gold paint and finished off with a satin ribbon bow.

each cone before it is anchored to the circle by slipping
the wire or string down between the scales of the cone, at
its base. The string is secured with several knots, or the
wire with several firm twists. For this type of work I use
nylon florist string but you may prefer florist spool wire.

The design may be started at any point on the circle by
attaching the first cone to the frame with the remaining
end of either string or wire. Successive cones are similarly
attached until the circle is completed. Cones may be placed
all in one direction around the circle or faced symmetri-
cally on either side, meeting at top and bottom. Graduated
sizes form more interesting patterns than those of all one
size. You may add a bow of ribbons but a well-made wreath
needs no embellishment.

The actual work of fastening is done on a flat surface
but from time to time the wreath should be hung and
viewed from a distance to see if the design is developing
satisfactorily and the outline of the circle forming properly.
In any wreath all of its design materials should conform
to the outline of the frame.

Garlands.   Garlands are fun to make and cones can be
combined with all sorts of other dried plants. The pieces
are attached to a double thickness of clothesline or rope,
which acts as a base. After making a loop in one end,
anchor it to something stationary before attaching the

39. CHRISTMAS SWAG

Here cones of various sizes are attached to ribbons and
hung from a big bright green bow to make a simple and
delightful Christmas decoration.

Robert Sc

pieces with the string or wire, which has previously been secured to each plant. It is important to choose dried plants which are easy to wire or tie. Small pieces, like acorns, nuts or seed pods, may be grouped together and attached as a unit. Such decorations are far more attractive if they have a rhythmic pattern and cones are excellent for this while other plants placed at intervals act as centers of interest. Arched doorways, staircases or over mantels are good places for this kind of decoration.

Cone Swag. Swags of cones are easily made by cutting 1"-wide ribbon into half a dozen varying lengths and attaching a cone to each length. Knot the opposite ends together securely, leaving a loop for hanging. Place a large bow, of wider ribbon of the same color, at the top to add an effective finishing touch. Red ribbon is the popular choice but brown or dark green gives a more subtle result. Similarly, 3 large western cones can be made into a swag. This decoration is easy enough for anyone to make and it has many uses in the home. (See Illustration 39.)

Other Dried Plant Wreaths. Tradition may say that a wreath should be made of greens but with the trend of the past few years toward decorations of a more permanent nature, many other kinds of materials are being used. Dried

40. FASCINATING CONES

Cones from Pinyon, Jeffrey, Ponderosa, White Pine and Douglas Fir trees are combined with White Pine branches in a washed copper urn to make a traditional Christmas design.

bert Scharff

plants meet the requirements of beauty and symmetry in wreaths and can be used for several holiday seasons, not just one.

For this kind of a wreath you need a base in which the stems of the dried plants may be inserted. When green, any type of thin branch may be bent into a circle or oval without breaking. During the summer, forms can be constructed with branches of shrubs such as Forsythia, Privet, Lilac or Scotch Broom, or with some vines. Make 3 or 4 circles or ovals of branches, overlap and tie the ends of each branch for a length of 2″, then lay 1 circle or oval on top of another, staggering the joinings, and tie them all together securely with string. After the frame has dried for 3 or 4 weeks add a layer of Sphagnum Moss and cover with florist or waxed paper. Both the moss and paper are held to the branches by wrappings of lightweight string to form a firm foundation into which the dried plants may be inserted.

The following are suggested ideas for this type of wreath:

A delightful combination can be formed by using Artemisia and Pearly Everlasting as a main-design material. It may be kept neutral with Bayberries and silver ribbon or brightened with chartreuse, fuchsia or lavender Christmas-tree balls and ribbon.

A wreath made with clusters of red Sumac is most unusual and needs no other accent to be decorative.

For a different kind of a wreath use varying shades of dried Dock accented by crests of red Celosia and a rust-colored ribbon bow.

Any of the colored Statices can be combined with painted cones and Strawflowers for an effective wreath.

A long oval wreath will reflect a quaint lavender-and-old-lace feeling. One combination I like is to make dried Artemisia the basic cover for a 30″ oval, adding lavender Heather, pink and lavender Statice, rose Celosia and Strawflowers all around the oval and introducing several groups of Honesty for a touch of shining whiteness. The wreath is intertwined with 3″ lavender ribbon culminating in a many-looped bow at the top.

For a tailored wreath of dried leaves you will need a solid circle 2″ to 3″ wide and 14″ to 16″ in diameter cut from plywood, Masonite or heavy cardboard. Spiral-wind the circle with a double thickness of corsage tape, at 1″ intervals, under which to insert the dried leaves. It is a simple matter to tuck the stem of each leaf under the tape, overlapping each one until the circle is covered. You can use any dried leaf of medium size, such as Magnolia, Eucalyptus, Ivy, Lemon or Rhododendron. The leaves may be left natural or lightly sprayed with gold, silver or colored paint after the wreath is finished.

Living Room. In the living room it is wiser to concentrate on one or two attractive decorations rather than to crowd the room with many. Give your best efforts to the mantel, for Santa enjoys gaiety and color for his stocking filling! Any of the wreaths I've mentioned can be hung above the fireplace and because of their decorative properties little else is required. A cone wreath looks exceptionally well against wood paneling and if you wish you may frame it with a larger evergreen wreath. Wreaths of dried leaves fit into modern settings while a long oval provides a rich decoration for Victorian furnishings.

When a mirror hangs above the mantel its reflective properties should be taken into consideration. A garland draped gracefully over a mantel mirror may be caught here and there with color and shiny Christmas-tree balls are especially good for this. For a crystal, gold or silver candelabrum on a mantel, a grouping of suitably colored dried plants at its base is adequate. One simple idea is to use several bunches of long-stemmed tiny Strawflowers, all one color, tie them with a graceful bow and lay them at the base of the candlestick on a spray of evergreens. Ceramic angels, choir boys or carol singers are always appropriate accents.

For Christmas dress up the occasional or coffee table with a small arrangement. There are hundreds of ideas you can use. A Santa's boot makes an unusual container for small white branches and candy canes. Cellophane-wrapped candies or lollipops can be wired together and grouped as flowers in small arrangements. A large plastic snowball or a small basket are other ideas for containers as well as small pieces of milk glass or silver.

One of the many beautiful Madonna figurines on the mantel, or other suitable place, will serve as a reminder of the meaning of Christmas. You can give the figure a feeling of dignity by using a large disk or circle as a background. Do not destroy the beauty of your figurine or its spiritual quality by too much material or garish overornamentation. Select dried plants carefully to blend with your figurine and dramatize them with white, gold or silver paint. Desert Holly, which remains white when dried, is lovely with an all-white Madonna. Angel's Wings (skeletonized leaves) arranged in a semicircle would be in harmony with many figurines.

The gaily trimmed Christmas tree is a focal point in many homes and the packages under its branches are always a joy to behold. No matter how small a gift may be, if it is wrapped with an individual touch it will be remembered. Fancy paper and ribbon are usual but for that something extra add dried plants. Small seed pods, cones or nuts, or bits of branches, vines or leaves will all blend with colored papers. Milkweed pods, painted red, will form Poinsettia-like flowers to use on top of a package. The individual scales of a large cone can be used to make attractive designs. Brown, white or chartreuse paper, gold ribbon and cones brushed with gold are a classic combination.

Whether young or old every woman loves wearing a corsage during the holiday season, so why not tie a gay, petite one in the bow of your Christmas packages? They are easily made by the method previously described, the cost is negligible and the combinations endless. Nature has a large supply of materials for this purpose and you may add any of the smaller seasonal trimmings for a bright touch. Colored pipe cleaners, small bells or miniature balls are all possibilities. Fashion each one as your fancy dictates but always add a perky bow of ribbon.

Every family has a holiday habit or annual custom that has grown into a tradition. In our home, for instance, each year a small plastic tree stands on the entrance hall table with many gay, small corsages on its branches. During the holiday season any guest arriving without a corsage receives one from the tree.

Small Trees.   Small artificial trees formed with dried plants are charming decorations for any room in the house and there is an infinite variety of smaller plants suitable for making these permanent decorations which can be used year after year. You will have fun dreaming up ideas for these trees as they can be entirely traditional or daringly modern.

The design may be made of only one kind of dried plant or you may prefer an assortment of cones, nuts and seed pods. (See Illustration 41.) While on the West Coast, I observed many artfully constructed trees, some made with Strawflowers in the daintiest of colors, and others of brilliant hue with nuts wrapped in bright cellophane. These ideas are worth trying.

Tree forms are easy to construct and may be made in one of these three shapes:

41. STYLIZED TREE

Assorted small seed pods, cones, nuts and leaves on a Styrofoam base make an attractive small Christmas tree. This one was sprayed first with white paint and then lightly with gold paint and "glitter" and the whole finished off with a gold ribbon bow.

Boutrelle-Seveck

A triangular, flat surface—1½ to twice as high as wide—of pasteboard or plywood, with the plants glued on one side.

A cone-shaped wire frame with the plant pieces fastened to the form.

A large ball of Styrofoam with the design pieces pushed into the ball.

Any of these types should be mounted on a wooden dowel, representing the trunk, to support the decorative portion and anchor the dowel to a base or in a container. Triangular or conical shapes look well on a square dowel and a wood base but a container is better suited to the ball shapes. A flower pot is excellent if painted to complement the tree's design and then filled with clay or plaster of Paris to hold the dowel firmly.

Last year I made a pair of most effective trees (inspired by the rose trees of France) using a large ball of Styrofoam, 7″ in diameter, for each tree shape. After closely covering the Styrofoam with Sweet Gum Balls, I mounted each tree on a dowel pin ½″ in diameter by pushing the pin into the Styrofoam. The other end of the dowel I secured in a square, quart-size, plastic freezer box, with plaster of Paris. I sprayed gold paint over all parts—Sweet Gum Balls, dowel and box, and attached a large, gold metallic bow, with ends trailing onto the table, to the under side of each ball with a colored pipe cleaner. These are easy, practical and make stunning decorations.

Dining Room. The decoration on your dining table is important and while it should express the seasonal spirit, it must conform to the room and table service. Perhaps you can use the traditional red and green but another color combination may be more appropriate. One dining room I know well is lovely each year with white and silver plants and pink balls. When in doubt as to what to use, choose the "White Christmas" theme, because it blends with almost everything and is sparkling, festive and highly suggestive of the season. Foam plastic, with its snowy whiteness, is an excellent base upon which to build many kinds of white decorative pieces. One of the following suggestions may help to make your table a memorable one:

Select, whiten and arrange graceful, leafless branches into a pattern in a block of foam. Decorate with small white ornaments, bows or whatever else you may fancy. To soften the harshness of the foam, add some white leaves or bits of evergreens at the base.

Insert a series of tall white candles in a long narrow piece of foam and group white glittered cones and leaves or bits of evergreens at the base.

Fill two glass chimneys or hurricane lamps with white plants. Interesting variations are possible with tree ornaments, in one of the new soft shades of lavender, pink, blue or chartreuse.

Fashion a tree on a ball of foam, as previously described. A pair of white trees, with gold or silver ribbon, is a handsome decoration.

Stunning table decorations can be made by glamourizing dried plants with gold or silver metallic paint. You will hear expressions of surprise as your guests recognize a pod, leaf or vegetable in the table piece.

If you wish to put your design in a container, paint the plants first.

If you wish to keep the design low and lay it on the table, use a piece of chicken wire and secure the plants to it with metallic thread. Construct the design in a graceful, free-flowing manner and give it an interesting silhouette outline. Paint the entire design after it is completed.

You will find that a mirror with 2 or 3 large bunches of gold or silver grapes produces a lavish effect. Bunches of grapes can be fashioned from large Italian Chestnuts, by forcing heavy dark-colored thread through their smaller ends with a large needle. Thread, group and knot 7 or 8 together and leave enough of an end on the thread to tie 3 or 4 of these groups into a large bunch. Paint the nuts after they are bunched and, for accent, while painting include a few dried leaves like Shallon, Magnolia, Ivy or Eucalyptus.

If you prefer to use other nuts, such as Pecans or Walnuts it will be necessary to use a red-hot pin or needle to penetrate the hard shell and make a tiny hole. Dip the end of a stiff piece of wire in glue, insert it in the hole and allow it to dry before the nuts are grouped and painted.

Glowing candles are a traditional part of any Christmas table setting. Today, candles come in many wonderful shapes from handmade to molded forms of trees, angels or animals. Candle holders which are used throughout the year take on a festive air when garnished with decorations. However, to avoid the hazard of fire, either keep the candles at a safe distance from dried plants or protect the flame with a glass chimney or hurricane lamp. Footed, large beer glasses are excellent holders for short fat candles.

Kitchen. The kitchen is a much-frequented place during the holidays and should not be overlooked while decorating. Whatever your kitchen décor, here is a golden opportunity to do something original and the following suggestions should help to make it a more cheerful spot while holiday menus are prepared:

Kitchen articles make wonderful containers. A shiny new funnel, hung on a nail, is extremely effective with a few dried plants and bright touches. A pair of wicker baskets are excellent for twin window sills. Even so common a thing as a bright red or a green dustpan makes a delightful container if inverted and filled with red and green plants. Copper utensils or wooden bowls are charming with gray, red and brown plants. One sensational combination is to use two new tin cake pans, one inverted as a stand and the other to hold the decorative materials. A shower of colored kitchen gadgets or candy canes tied with ribbons and a few dried plants adds a distinctive touch. I even go so far as to put a simple swag with cowbells and a red oilcloth bow on my back door so that the tradespeople know that Christmas is all through our house. This year plan something new and different for your kitchen!

Painting Christmas Decorations. You can do wonderful things to dried plants with paint and they can be prepared well in advance and quickly assembled when the holiday rush is on. All plants must be clean, dried, tied or wired before painting. Chapter 15 discussed painting dried plants but the following are a few suggestions especially for Christmas decorations:

Semigloss paints produce a better effect than high-gloss enamels. White poster paint or shoe polish will dry to a dull finish in a short time. Aluminum paint may be used for silver effects. For metallic paints a spray is much easier to handle. However, you may find that a brush is better for applying paint to small pieces. Leaves need only be painted on one side but seed pods may require two coats of paint.

Sparkle and glitters add a fairylike appearance to dried plants and should be sprinkled on while the paint is wet. Harlequin is my favorite glitter and it is lovely on white poster-painted plants. If you wish to use sparkle on metallic paint, it is best to let the paint dry and then cover it with a coat of colorless shellac or colorless nail enamel, before adding the sparkle. Many unpainted plants are attractive with a coat of colorless nail polish sprinkled with glitter. You might try pink nail enamel and harlequin glitters.

You will find that, except for white, all painted pods, branches or cones may be stored in a box without deterioration. Those painted white may show discoloration as many of the paints tend to turn yellow. Sun and air or soap and water may bring back the whiteness but it is simpler to repaint and be certain of snowy whiteness in your decorations.

Christmas is particularly for children and they should be allowed to assist with the preparation of decorations. They love to help gather and paint materials and if properly directed can be a real help. Nothing is more alluring than putting on old clothes and playing in wet paint. Working together as a family adds meaning to Christmas decorations and it is important to give children precious memories that they can cherish all through their lives.

Appendix

Where to Buy Dried Plants

Your local florist usually has in his stock some dried plants but the following list may help you to find special items.

ART TROPICAL FOLIAGE COMPANY
Box 755
Palmetto, Florida

Foliage suitable for drying

CAMPBELL'S
1914—10th Street
Bremerton, Washington

Cones, seed pods and other dried plants

DISTINCTIVE DRIFTWOOD
Route #1, Box 79
Brookings, Oregon

West Coast driftwood

DRUKE'S   Various kinds of dried plants
Box 36
Carmel Valley, California

FLORAL ART   Some types of dried plants
Box 394
Highland Station
Springfield, Massachusetts

JACK SULLIVAN'S   All types of dried plants
4000 Broadway
Everett, Washington

MONTEREY PENINSULA   Small and miniature dried ma-
CRAFT   terials
Box 706
Monterey, California

PALM VALLEY RANCH   All types of dried plants
Box 70
Palm Springs, California

RAMONT'S FLORAL ARTS   Foliage, pods and grasses
STUDIOS
Box 667
Yucaipa, California

WESTERN TREE CONES   Specializes in cones
1925 Brooklane
Corvallis, Oregon

Index